Vertigo

THE LIVING DEAD MAN POEMS

Also by Marvin Bell

Marvin Bell

Vertigo

The Living Dead Man Poems

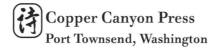 Copper Canyon Press
Port Townsend, Washington

Copyright 2011 by Marvin Bell

Printed in the United States of America

Cover art: Morris Graves, *Space Age Mandala #2,* 1977. Watercolor, tempera, and pastel on paper. Sixteen inches diameter. Courtesy of the Morris Graves Foundation.

Copper Canyon Press is in residence at Fort Worden State Park in Port Townsend, Washington, under the auspices of Centrum. Centrum is a gathering place for artists and creative thinkers from around the world, students of all ages and backgrounds, and audiences seeking extraordinary cultural enrichment.

LIBRARY OF CONGRESS CATALOGING-IN-PUBLICATION DATA

Bell, Marvin, 1937–
Vertigo : the living dead man poems/Marvin Bell.
    p. cm.
ISBN 978-1-55659-376-5 (pbk. : alk. paper)
1. Title.
PS3552.E52V47 2011
811'.54 — dc22

                                                    2011001406

9 8 7 6 5 4 3 2 FIRST PRINTING

Copper Canyon Press
Post Office Box 271
Port Townsend, Washington 98368
www.coppercanyonpress.org

Dorothy, Nathan, Jason
Leslie, Colman, Aileen
Frank & Carole, Al, Pete & Lani

Grateful acknowledgment is made to the plucky editors of the following publications in which these poems first appeared:

The American Poetry Review; Arch Literary Journal; Arroyo Literary Review; Audemus; Border Senses; Boulevard; Breathe: 101 Contemporary Odes; Camoupedia: A Compendium of Research on Art, Architecture and Camouflage; The Coachella Review; Crazyhorse; Cutthroat; Denver Quarterly; Ecotone; Electronic Poetry Review; The Fiddlehead; The Georgia Review; The Gettysburg Review; Green Mountains Review; The Iowa Review; Make; New Poets of the American West; The New Yorker; /One/; Phainomai; Pleiades; Poetry Miscellany; Poetry Northwest; Prairie Schooner; Projector; Rattle; Rhino; The Southern Review; Visiting Dr. Williams: Poems Inspired by the Life and Work of William Carlos Williams; We Wanted To Be Writers; Whiteout: Dead Man Poems by Marvin Bell in Response to Photographs by Nathan Lyons.

"The Book of the Dead Man (Collaboration)" was mounted for the Born Installation & Performance *The Eight Essential Ingredients,* Richard Hugo House, Seattle, 2006.

The point of philosophy is to start with something so simple as not to seem worth stating, and to end with something so paradoxical that no one will believe it.

BERTRAND RUSSELL

When my daughter was about seven years old, she asked me one day what I did at work. I told her I worked at the college — that my job was to teach people how to draw. She stared at me, incredulous, and said, "You mean they forget?"

HOWARD IKEMOTO

CONTENTS

Vertigo

THE LIVING DEAD MAN POEMS

THE BOOK OF THE DEAD MAN (THE ALLEYS)

Live as if you were already dead.
ZEN ADMONITION

1. About the Dead Man and the Alleys

The dead man, bowling, hit the head pin.

Thinking he was dead-on, he was, it was the sign of the times, the
        human condition, his wanting the wrong thing.

With the one pin knocked out, the dead man was once again in a
        life of dichotomy.

Now he looks at the 7-10 split and wonders, which side?

He can't help seeing the split as life and death, chance and no
        chance, public courage and inner cowardice.

In the classroom, the tenth frame would be final, the eleventh a
        probation, and the twelfth an afterlife.

Here, if the dead man tries to bounce the seven off the wall and
        across the alley, it will take dumb luck, it could happen.

The pin boys have their legs up, why not try.

If the dead man tries instead to slice the far edge of the ten and
        skitter it across, it will be once-in-a-lifetime or the gutter.

Here, too, is the human condition he remembers, writ in hand
        dryers, rental shoes, tenpins, duckpins, candlepins.

The raucous, shiny leagues filling the lanes, the monorail of balls
        thudding up into line.

And the chart of boxes, for the one inclined toward fractions
        and addition.

The beer frames, the whiskey frames, the turning away after a roll
        and looking over one's shoulder to see if of course...

2. More About the Dead Man and the Alleys

Now the ball hooks sharply, and the pins dance.

The asymmetrical core is something like our new selves.

The dead man has known the stone balls of kegel, the pre-modern ironwood, the hard rubber before resin, urethane, and particle balls.

He has seen the weight the world put upon the shoulders of these new bowlers, even as the weapons grew lighter.

He can sense the new ball picking up oil as it rolls.

He can see the ball hook sharply into the pocket as if it knows.

The dead man's human and inhuman conditions have melded.

Someone else may not know what it was to be the pin boy hurrying to dodge the impatient early roller and earn tips.

There are perfect games galore now, is it still bowling?

The dead man knows that a new tool, like a new cadence, is a new idea.

He didn't have to be an Imagist to see what's up.

He didn't have to be a Cubist or a Futurist to see what was coming.

It still sounds like a wingding, it still feels like a jamboree, it's the heavy ball headed for you-know-what.

THE BOOK OF THE DEAD MAN (ANUBIS)

Live as if you were already dead.

1. About the Dead Man and Anubis

The dead man, considering, was asked, "When is the right time?"

What if one were whisked away too quickly to be missed, not even
        the smell after a lightning strike, not even the mist of a
        teakettle just turned off.

Ah, but the dead man is more resilient than the grass, more
        recollected than the jalopy of first romance, more encrypted
        than the crypt.

He outlasts the red dross of old blood.

He outlasts the clockwork, he lengthens the leap years.

The dead man may lie safely under a palm tree, or cross the
        barbed wire.

He cannot be harmed by a coconut, he is not a target on
        the battlefield.

Now he is beyond both the local and the larger, out of range,
        calmly of a piece with gravity and the genuflecting universe.

Let him furrow his brow, it doesn't matter.

Let him wrinkle like the pelt of a cheetah or bloodhound,
        either way.

He survives any comparison.

All time is the right time for the dead man, but in time you may
        miss him.

2. More About the Dead Man and Anubis

The dead man will find you.

He has befriended the weigher of souls and keeper of tombs.

He is the I-Thou of what matters for a while, then less.

Hence, the dead man repeats his pleasures in memory.

He loves the swish of the broom, the crease in the bedsheet.

He hears as well the music of the rattletrap as that of the wind.

He feels the weight of *more,* the heapings of the world.

He calls the pot black, he lounges till noon in his reading garb.

The dead man outlasts the low sky, the soggy, the arid, the
       freezing, the sweltering.

He has vaulted the horizon, he has dispersed the material.

Here come the worms, is it time?

Turn here to see the dead man riding in the rumble seat.

THE BOOK OF THE DEAD MAN (THE ARCH)

Live as if you were already dead.

1. About the Dead Man and the Arch

In the curvature of space, in the ox yoke of industry, half-
      encircled by the arm of the rainbow or earthly in the curled
      palm of an open hand, the dead man lives ahead and behind.
The dead man's back arches as he bends to see or leans back
      in submission.
The dead man has ridden within the hollow arch.
He has scratched at the stone arch, feeling for the Etruscans.
He thinks the arch may follow the path of their lost language.
The dead man sees in the arch an incomplete zero, a footless oval,
      a hoof-guard, French arches triumphant, arches written in
      Utah by erosion.
Arthritic fingers are arches, and the flood-curled covers of art
      books, and the torso of a kneeling prisoner.
In such manner is dead man's geometry displaced from purity of
      thought, even as the age echoes with the latest "Eureka!"
Oh, purity of intention, beauties of foresight, and the fork in
      the road.
For it was the divergent that sent one uphill or down.
It was the creation of options that sent the brain reeling, the
      economy spiraling, and invented mixed feelings.
Then came the arch of architecture, which limned entry and exit,
      the yes and no, the business of going in or staying out.
Every arch is academic, for the arch that props a bridge or roofs a
      tunnel is a theoretical proof.

2. More About the Dead Man and the Arch

Ogee or reverse ogee, three-centered or segmental, triangular,
    equilateral, parabolic, the shouldered, the elliptical.
(About lakes, Auden wrote, "Just reeling off their names is ever
    so comfy.")
And his favorite, the "rampant round."
So doth the arch aspire from the ground up.
What better can this life be described than as "rampant round."
The dead man has stood on the arches of his feet, minding his fate.
He has fallen in with ideas with dirt on their shoes, arch-like.
He has worn out the merely sensational, that does not arc.
The dead man is not arch, but loves the arch as a geezer at the end
    of the Greek alphabet lifts a tumbler of ouzo.
Yes, the arch trembles at the chance to be both the beginning and
    the end.
The dead man, like you, entered through an archway of effects.
Everything is water if he looks hard, it is all a line over the
    horizon, a circle spreading outward from its core, a tilted
    parallelogram leaning on a wormhole, it can be the floor he
    falls through.
It is what he passed through and under.

THE BOOK OF THE DEAD MAN (ARROYO)

Live as if you were already dead.

1. About the Dead Man and the Arroyo

The dead man blesses the new arroyo.

The dead man knows that the arroyo is a gulf and a gulch, a gap
and a gorge.

He has seen words fall into the abyss.

He has clamored on the way down and gasped on the way up,
gripping the sides of makeshift handholds.

He has himself carelessly tossed what he meant to say over the rim.

He has both feared the edge and regretted his distance.

For it was in the topographic scheme of the art to propose to a
muse in the dark, and who knew?

The long picaresque adventure of trying to say a life took place on
a rim trail.

Turning back in sight of the waterfall… there came the two wolves
where there were not thought to be wolves.

They were dead ahead, coming, and the dead man sought a stick
but in vain.

Was the dead man making this up, was he the lie that tells the truth?

Then the dead man saw the wolves split up and go down and
reemerge high on each side, watching.

Now when the rain comes and rises in the arroyo, the dead man
wades in memory.

He of the wolves in the wild, he of the well bucket, he of the
ragged creeks, he of the waters within him is of a piece with
all that washes away.

Pour your heart into the dry arroyo to be nourished and run off.

Empty your mind into the parched crevasse to be filled
    and dispersed.
All of it will have its moment.
You can bring it up.

2. More About the Dead Man and the Arroyo

The dead man supposes he sees the sun rise from a promontory at
      the canyon.
He is able to do this because he did it.
To remember, for the dead man, is to do it all again.
The dead man can dance as if for the first time because he hears
      again a new song.
He can read new words in the shape of old ones, there is a
      crackling on the paper as they are born.
Were it not a planet with a molten core, the dead man could not
      stir things up so.
The dead man has blurred the edge so that now the arroyo is the
      dead man's mountain ridge.
The indentations in the walls of the arroyo are the dead man's
      foothills.
So that all that was thought to be descending, now ascends, and
      here he comes.
You cannot step on his speech, but the dead man's lingo will get in
      your head.
When there is no more paper, no ashes, no balsa wings, no feather
      blanket, no cloud cover, no omen, then upstream and
      downstream are the same stream.
When the rains come, when the squatter pebbles are evicted, when
      the flood is born and the wash is awash.
The dead man has been reading from underneath.
He has peered up through the four elements.

He has peeked between the flames and into the cracks.
He has peeled the dew and held his breath.
What better for the dead man than an arroyo, a chasm, hollows
      and ravines?
The dead man stands down to see up.

THE BOOK OF THE DEAD MAN (BIG EYES)

Live as if you were already dead.

1. About the Dead Man and Big Eyes

Would it have been news if space aliens had landed?
Late-night radio said it was old news, embedded in Stonehenge,
    crop circles, sky lights, the Pyramids.
The dead man was up late listening to the reports of space travelers.
Think of the dead man as a big head with huge eyes.
And the dead man's fingers carving disembodied scribblings.
The dead man cannot span an octave, and he types with two
    fingers, he has to look.
Like a camera, he squints to lengthen the depth of his field and
    bring the future into focus.
The dead man's eyes have seen too little or too much, it depends.
When the dead man opened the blinds and looked out, he saw
    farther into himself.
It widened his eyes, it dropped his jaw, it made his hands flutter
    to flee.

2. More About the Dead Man and Big Eyes

If the prisms of the eyes were not the prisoners of the brain.

If the eyes were not the windows of the soul.

If the soul were not incarcerated in the notion of a definite shape.

With every quantum measurement, the dead man is expelled from
      another universe.

Hence, he is multiversal, inside and out.

If you don't want to talk about it, the dead man understands.

When the Dog Star shines in his eye, the dead man blinks.

A time exposure to record it would take centuries, and he blinks.

If the soul was an eye, if the window was a door, if the brain was
      as plastic as space.

The planet will not be leaving without the dead man.

THE BOOK OF THE DEAD MAN (BOOMERANG)

Live as if you were already dead.

1. About the Dead Man and the Boomerang

The dead man stands still, waiting for the boomerang to —
     you know.
He hears the words of philosophers ricochet among chasms and
     disappear in the far away.
His scent goes forth, his old skin, hair and nails, and he spits, too.
He leans forward to look backward, and the ancient world reappears.
It is the beginning, when mountains, canyons and seas were new,
     before the moon had eyes, before paper, before belief.
Any words he utters now are souvenirs of the future.
They will be meant to keep a pestilence from returning.
They will be meant to string together a path to follow in the dark.
The dead man will ask who you are fighting for, do you know, will
     it come back to haunt you?
He will ask about the taste of ashes, he will ask if you remember.

2. More About the Dead Man and the Boomerang

The dead man's army swept the battlefield and brought the
war home.

It was a time of troop surges and redactions, leaks and fire
starters, a time of bush-league government.

The dead man's zest for words went local, it came home to gravel
underfoot and mud under the eaves.

The dead man knows that all invasions are boomerangs, ask
Napoleon, it rains on every parade.

The dead man fingers those who will be revisiting the wars they
began.

He high-steps to pass over the casualties who left their thirst on
the sand and their bones in the caves.

The dead man, too, is waist deep in gore, his belly full, his balance
sheet bleak, but no deadbeat, he will be heard from.

The boomerang effect has been building from war to war,
campaign to campaign, unit to unit.

A clicking of dog tags.

An army of medics and morticians.

THE BOOK OF THE DEAD MAN (BORDERS)

Live as if you were already dead.

1. About the Dead Man and Borders

The dead man is an immigrant, an exile, a local and a foreigner.

He came across the dry border or the ocean.

He walked, he rode, he sailed, he flew, he traveled miles on
     his knees.

He may have come by way of shadows, moving only in darkness.

He may have traveled without shoes, with little food or water,
     but still he carried his story, his temperature, his
     elemental rhythms.

Now the dead man feels a chill as the barricades rise.

He has the past in view, its clues, its nuances and hints, perfumed
     by a wisp of safety.

The dead man has proffered his passport for close inspection.

When the dead man rode a bus from Slovenia to Italy, the guards
     dragged his luggage from the bay.

And when he took the train to return, a sea-legged policeman
     yanked his suitcase from the overhead.

It was he whom the man in the dark coat followed around the
     dissident art show come to Venice from Russia.

What is it about the dead man that made him a target before the
     antiwar events had even begun?

The dead man can still feel the fist that missed, passing close by
     where he stopped to eat in the tavern.

He has known the armies to conscript fathers and mothers.

He has seen them composting war's fodder.

He has seen the massed volunteers whose forerunners had to run
     to his country for their lives.

If there was enough time between a wink and a nod, perhaps
someone would replace the Welcome sign that was
torn down.
If there were dollars to go around, if there were health galore and
ambiguous tea leaves, then the dancing might last longer.
If it had not been necessary to crawl or duckwalk or roll over.
The dead man does not know where to place the line between here
and there, them and us, like and dislike.
The dead man hath married the haves and have-nots till death do
they part.
The dead man lives on the life-and-death border, above which he
hovers, looking to this side and that.
The dead man is a realist.

2. More About the Dead Man and Borders

The dead man does not take sides.

He has crossed the big river, he has joined in, he has worn the
        lone Star of David and the ankh, the good luck rubber
        band, the medical alert.

He has carried his address in his pocket, just in case.

The dead man knows that every homeland dies and is reincarnated
        and tries to recover its past.

Look at his struggles to be more like this one or that one.

The dead man, too, was born into his bias.

The dead man, like you, has been skinned alive by the historians
        who needed parchment to write the story of the victors.

The dead man knows the drill.

He knows where to stand to be let go.

He knows how to blend in, he waves the übernationalist flag on
        the holiday, he scans the frontier.

There must be something about the dead man that raises suspicion.

The dead man's skin is of many colors, perhaps that's a red flag.

The dead man speaks the languages some take for code.

The dead man limps a bit, which reminds them.

The memory of an injury makes them crazy to see the dead man
        limping or grimacing or just breathing hard.

The dead man does not want to see the aftermath of the explosion,
        to stir the ashes after the fire, or pull the victims from the
        rubble over and over throughout his nights, but he does.

The dead man is free to be fatally sensitive, he has been left to
 his feelings, his blubbering, his inner aches, his embedded
 limitations.
The dead man is a realist with reasons, does that help, can he stay?
Will the dead man cross over with last words?
The dead man has friends all over the world who will hide him.
The dead man has invisibility on his side, so where is he?

THE BOOK OF THE DEAD MAN (THE BOULEVARD)

Live as if you were already dead.

1. About the Dead Man on the Boulevard

The dead man was out walking on the boulevard when he
    looked up.
There, over his head, was the famous silver lining.
The street was as wide as the wingspans of four turkey vultures,
    he could look up and up.
He understood that the silver lining was related to the lateness of
    the hour.
He had eaten the chocolate kisses, he had used up the leftovers,
    he had ordered takeaway.
When he walks, the dead man reaches beyond his arms, he strides
    beyond his step, he unscrews the vise of three dimensions.
Here is the silver lining of tomorrow's sun at storm's edge.
(Did you guess that the dead man is out walking in a thin rain?
In the gray drops falling that blush when they hit the pavement?)
The dead man can do this in his sleep, in cloud cities, in stories he
    populates with people who also walk.

2. More About the Dead Man on the Boulevard

For the dead man, the world enlarges as he walks.
He is unable to look straight ahead, he catalogues the window
      dressers, he sets the mannequins in motion.
(Did I mention the light rain clearly enough for you to see it?)
Go walk the boulevard when the young couples are circling and
      the mothers watch their unmarried offspring like hawks.
When the late light alchemizes the air, when the sun falls into
      the net.
Each sensory selection uses up the dead man until he moves on.
It happens in a jiffy, in a flash, in a tick, in what youth calls a sec,
      it is all and everything for as long as anything.
If it were not for the lateness of the hour, everything he sees
      would be too much.
At the café, he dispenses the advice of one who has hiked the past.
The dead man's thoughts lengthen his years, straighten his bowed
      legs, and oil his lumbering, stumbling, strolling and
      skipping walkabouts.

THE BOOK OF THE DEAD MAN (THE BOX)

Live as if you were already dead.

1. About the Dead Man and the Box

When the dead man wants to deaden his brain, he surfs the
      channels.

He rides the Bonsai Pipeline of twenty-four-hour cable news.

He hears the field reporter, covering a death, pun on a grave
      experience.

He sees the reporter push a microphone into the face of the widow.

And the basketball sideliners asking players about giving 110%.

The dead man is 50% half-involved.

He thinks TV news is one long Jay Letterman, David Leno show.

He thinks the public forums have been Oprah-sized.

The pancake, the wigs, the stagy confessions...

He sees the ads for bad drugs and rollover cars and the
      disclaimers that flit past under low fares.

He hears the claims of the Ponzi brokerages, the gold hawkers
      and the latest minting of memorial coins.

His ears are filled with the incessant hawking of the latest murder,
      mayhem and marketing.

He switches among the evening reports of the three major
      networks: the stylish, the sentimental and the earnest.

The dead man has seen the Johnny-come-latelies come and go and
      the good one-in-a-million.

He remembers ugly Joe Pyne's wooden leg, quirky Ernie Kovacs'
      cigar, cackly Steverino Allen's fedora.

Now he labors to tell a thousand young actors apart.

He hears humor where there was none.

2. More About the Dead Man and the Box

The dead man lives in the flickering tube-light of rampant
      capitalism.
But if he wades through the smog of ads, there may be a late-night
      movie.
Casablanca, Bagdad Cafe, My Favorite Year, The Stunt Man,
      Lawrence of Arabia, Slap Shot, Matinee, Duets, Without a
      Clue, Brassed Off, Men with Brooms, Funny Bones...
Like lives, they end, each in turn, while warfare is serialized.
The dead man finds interstices in the American experience where
      people live who would never sell their story.
The dead man knows that there was never any news,
      just information.
He watches the news for the latest candidate, the big mudslide,
      the endless weather, the car chases, the Amber Alerts, the
      evangelical, the pogroms and genocides, and the latest
      worldly laundry.
The bad tidings encase his heart so that no single hurt can break
      through the tidal analgesic of the daily news.
He struggles toward late night hoping for no more news.
Music, dancing, humor and repartee squeeze through the airwaves.
The dead man believes radio blooms inside his head, while TV
      dies on the skin of his eyeballs.
The dead man thinks the telly should light up at midnight.

THE BOOK OF THE DEAD MAN (CAMOUFLAGE)

Live as if you were already dead.

1. About the Dead Man and Camouflage

When the dead man wears his camouflage suit, he hides in
plain sight.

The dead man, in plain sight, disrupts the scene but cannot be seen.

His chocolate-chip-cookie shirt mimics the leaves in a breeze.

His frog-skin dress, his bumpy earth nature leave us lost and
alone, his mottled apparel sends us in circles.

His displacements distract and disabuse us, he is a slick beguiler.

Everything the dead man does is a slight disruption of normality.

He is the optical trickster, the optimum space-saver, the one to
watch for.

He is of a stripe that flusters convention, he is the one to watch
out for.

That we thought him gone only proves his wily knowledge.

The dead man has lain unseen among the relics of embalmed time.

He was always here, always there, right in front of us, timely.

For it was not in the dead man's future to be preserved.

It was his fate to blend in, to appear in the form of, to become...

Now he lives unseen among the lilies, the pines, the sweet corn.

It was the dead man's native desire to appear not to be.

2. More About the Dead Man and Camouflage

The dead man knows that camouflage is all in the mind.

He has seen in the human need for shape the undoing of shape.

He has witnessed the displacement of up-and-down, across and
slantwise.

He has curled the straight lines and unbent the curves, he has split
the wishbone and painted outside the lines.

The dead man has undone the map by which to get there.

It is not what the dead man looks like, but what he no longer
resembles.

For he hath reappeared in no disguise but as himself.

Call him disheveled, call him disposed, call him shiftless, he is.

For he hath been made and remade in the form of his surroundings.

He hath become all things that he looketh like.

Hence, he has been stepped on by those who could not see him.

He has been knelt upon by those who looked in vain.

The dead man bestirs in a background that looked inert.

The dead man is the ultimate camouflage.

He is everywhere, but where is he?

THE BOOK OF THE DEAD MAN (COLLABORATION)

Live as if you were already dead.

1. About the Dead Man and Collaboration

When the dead man joins up, he monitors the monitors.

The dead man, enlisting, pictures the pictures.

He moves among the moving, wiggles among the squiggles, yes,
he laughs.

The dead man is part of a new language in the offshoot,
unpronounceable yet tip-of-the-tongue.

There will be birthing and splicing, fusing and fluxing, a Gabe and
a Jacob, a Scott and a Larry, two Stevens, one Anmarie,
and the dead man detecting.

He sees the trees morph into pixels, the text glue itself to the air.

Now hyperspace fills the room.

Now the dead man lives on, embedded in the universal retina.

Will universal collaboration create God?

Only the dead man has pictured it, seen it, absorbed it.

The dead man takes in sight and sound, stillness and movement.

Like the quantum cat, he can be in two places at once, he can
move and stay, he alone can be what you wanted and did
not want all in one.

There is no stopping the dead man, who is perpetual.

There is no cessation of the life force a-borning.

The dead man tunes in online and offline, from Earth and space.

Once launched, the sights and sounds, the signals and sense travel
through time, tidal waves without water.

2. More About the Collaborative Dead Man

The dead man is perforce an installation.
Buried or burned, hung up in the body lab, doled out to the organ
      banks, he is also rooted in memory.
In his disassembly he is assembled, in his dismantling he is
      established.
Now he is set among the trees and the leaves that paint the air.
Now his skeleton becomes the ridges and fissures of the planet.
His is the ultimate collaboration, the reciprocal to its nth, the
      true mutual.
He is a proponent of the big shebang theory.
The dead man is the past, present and future, an amalgamate of
      atoms and strings and the who-knows-what of bespectacled
      theorists.
Meanwhile, he wiggles among the squiggles, he mops up the
      washes, he rolls on the scrolls, he whirls within the whorls,
      he goofs in the gyres, yes he laughs and laughs, and yes he
      squirms among the worms.
He is the ready affiliate.
He is awash in the senses.
He lives among those who have mixed eyefuls and earfuls, oil and
      water, who have alchemized the elements and written in
      the pitch.
This now is the roadway of the dead man, united in every state.
The dead man shuffles his senses, he flicks, he riffles, he ruffles
      and rumples, he puckers and crinkles, he wrinkles, he
      scrunches, he stretches, and oh yes he struts a little, too.

Behold the dead man at the still point of a turning.
See the dead man painting by infinite numbers.

THE BOOK OF THE DEAD MAN (CONVERSATION)

Live as if you were already dead.

1. About the Dead Man's Conversations

The dead man hath spoken with Matthew Arnold about
    ignorant armies.
He hath cautioned Keats on the isolate love of beauty.
If there were ever Grecian odes on the shore, they were smashed
    in the general onslaught.
Like sand castles adrift in the idea of architecture, like bas-reliefs
    planed to the texture of papyrus, like rubber in acid, the
    repositories of beauty did not outlast the idea of them.
The dead man is of a mind, and a mind to, and his exploration has
    been in the places where an idea may fit.
It has been a long thrill in the dark for the dead man and friends.
The dead man is on the side of art but also on the side of
    artlessness.
Absent the blank page, the word must forever be muddied.
The words can be true only to one another, like Arnold's lovers —
    the ideal.
Well, says the dead man, what have we here?
It seems the dead man has caught the words in a compromising
    position.
This verbal interruptus is aquiver from circling an invisible vase
    where the lovers have been trying to catch one another.
Must poetry forever be anticipation and delayed gratification?
The dead man has been talking with T.S. Eliot about escaping
    one's personality, which he has.
And with Wallace Stevens about the mind in the act of finding
    what will suffice, which he has.

The dead man, too, can write the tautologies that cloak war
and torture.
But he no longer cottons to the aesthetic tilt of a head, the
legendary voice, the prophetic boom box or starlit ego.
Why should the dead man use up his life in the usual ways?
The dead man's poetry is not stone cold soup.

2. More About the Dead Man's Conversations

It was cold in the coffeehouse where the dead man met the editor.
The dead man had asked Henry James if there could be two
      congruent points of view.
He had challenged William James to a bout of automatic writing.
The dead man won the game of exquisite corpse when he folded
      the paper twice.
He wrote faster and faster, but he could not get down everything.
The engineers were of a mind to map a brain — an empty brain.
When the dead man and the editor met, it was in the early years of
      the Apocalypse.
That no one could conceive of everything had given the lie
      to prophecy.
It was a time when string theory was unraveling, when relativity
      had become absolute, when Gurdjieff's "all and everything"
      subsumed the cults, clans, castes, tribes and schools.
The dead man's papers had been overwritten.
It was up to the editor to select a sample.
The dead man has lived among remnants, shards, fragments,
      doubles and replicas, among lucky error and
      deliberate effect.
Like a snake, the dead man molts, leaving a whole skin now passé.
How shall the editor edit the seamless if not with scissors?
The dead man has been talking to James Joyce about not being
      there when his words end up new.
The dead man has been talking to Galileo about the law of falling
      bodies, which applies.

How shall the editor edit the perpetual or eternal if not
      with scissors?
The dead man's world is kaleidoscopic, it turns without stopping.
Say you knew him, but not what he was thinking.

THE BOOK OF THE DEAD MAN (THE CROSSING)

Live as if you were already dead.

1. About the Dead Man and the Crossing

The dead man hath been assigned to the children.

They stand on one side or the other, fidgeting, waiting to cross.

There will be a signal, a light, a flashing, and a dead man or
> woman in the middle of the street.

It is time to cross, says the dead man.

There are things to do so that you can do other things, says the
> dead woman.

The dead man remembers being an immortal child.

He recalls the daze of schooldays, the waiting to cross.

He, too, hurried through the stopped traffic to scuffle at recess.

He, too, watched the silhouettes through the frosted window of
> the classroom door after hours.

He, like you, felt the emptiness of the corridors.

He would take the senior trip to the Capitol and whisper under
> the dome.

It was long ago, and he was crossing without a guard.

He was not yet seething with ragged theories.

He curried desire, he lacked iridescence, he sank from failure.

He just wanted to get to the other side, like they said to.

2. More About the Dead Man and the Crossing

Clap quick, the immortal child is fast becoming the dead man.
The dead man who is alive and also dead.
He crosses repeatedly whatever there is to be crossed.
He shows up in the street before classes begin, stopping the cars.
He hurries the students to classes, but after school they hurry
      themselves themselves.
He stands in the street like a deciduous tree as they run past.
When the leaf blowers restart, the dead man knows what to do.
He may have tinnitus from the car horns, he may this day be
      scarlet from the chill, he may be fatter than last year.
Still, he is at peace with the one fact that most informs science,
      puzzles philosophy, and troubles medicine: that things end.
The dead man stands in the street, not letting the children cross
      just because they think they want to.
They are children, their lives are waiting.
The dead man, as a crossing guard, does more than required.
He is amplitude personified, he is the future withheld.
He waves, he beckons yes and no, he stops trouble in its tracks.
To the children, he is just arms and a rubber coat.

THE BOOK OF THE DEAD MAN (CUTTHROAT)

Live as if you were already dead.

1. About the Dead Man and the Cutthroat

The dead man steps guardedly around the fallen, picture the
    battlefields.
The arms and legs are the pickup sticks of war games.
Who were these unfortunates who couldn't move out of the way?
Were they the sons of senators, clad in legacy blazers?
Were they the daughters of governors, atop the cavalry of their
    thoroughbreds?
Here is why they cap the radio mic in foam or a stocking, no
    popping, no spitting.
They are cutthroat who stop for no one, some are politicos, some
    are commandos, some are little more than retail.
The dead man remembers the mom-and-pops driven from
    Main Street by loss leaders at the chains.
What are we to do in a world of absolutes the dead man rejected?
The dead man spat his experience at those with the knives, it
    was dangerous.

2. More About the Dead Man and the Cutthroat

The dead man would be of the primary cutthroat trout class, one
     of freshwater and not inclined to migrate.
Let the salmon climb ladders, let the salmon die in the gasp of the
     life force.
Let schools of salmon exhale to blow down the trees as they perish.
We little ones, like the cutthroat trout, we the meek, we shall
     inherit.
We will sputter with the hook in our mouth but say nothing more
     than spit.
Fishermen of the deep do not want our language, they live for
     the ocean.
The open sea is a cemetery, the open sea is a past century, the
     open sea is too big for us.
The river is where we live, the lake, the canal, wherever we can be
     at our throats with kisses or with knives.
It is not so far to one another that we cannot get there.
It is not so far to one another that we may not get there.

THE BOOK OF THE DEAD MAN (THE DARE)

Live as if you were already dead.

1. About the Dead Man and the Dare

The dead man edges toward the precipice because he dares.

He dares to wake the audience.

He is of a mind to taunt and defy, to provoke and to goad.

The dead man urges the stuntman to repeat his death-defying
spectacular.

He dares the trapeze artist and the wire walker to flaunt their
nonchalance.

He is of a mind to exploit the acrobatic.

Where in the lexicon of good government did threat and menace
replace courage?

The dead man is a reminder to the lawmakers.

It was dead men who won the revolution.

It was dead men who wrote the laws.

It was dead men who armed the citizenry that they might turn on
one another.

It was dead men who defended the cities, and it is dead men
whose names are etched in the town squares.

The dead man dares to tell you what you know you know.

The dead man would have dared more, had he known the outcome
of waiting.

To the dead man, existence is like a bungee on which he must fall
and rise, and fall again, until the distance is erased between
up and down.

It was a split-second decision to take the cord and jump.

The dead man was a thought that became tactile, became
palpable, some like to call him corporeal.

The dead man is the overarching presence, the coverall that
      let him kneel, the tarp that covered the weapons, the
      canvas bag, the muslin sail, the percale sheet, the cotton
      handkerchief into which he breathed.
Tell him you know.
Cover your mouth if you need to, but speak up.

2. More About the Dead Man and the Dare

The dead man has been afflicted by life, no complaint there.

The dead man does not make more of it than it was.

How best to call out the unjust and violent, the barons, the
      conglomerates, the cabals, the cartels and all who rise on
      the bent backs of others.

It is the dead man's place to call them out.

Everyone believes a dead man, and all men are dead men, we can
      get together and dismiss those who are daring us to.

The dead man says you know.

The dead man lives serenely in the backyards, in the surrounding
      farmlands, by the sides of ski trails and firebreaks, he is the
      one who will be coming from every direction.

The dead man's studies do not conclude, his decisions are not
      countermanded, the outcome of his being both here and
      gone can only mean that there will be daring.

The dead man has endowed daring in the arts but also in
      the streets.

He has fomented peace and made himself present on
      the battlefields.

He has placed himself in the way, who will step over him?

Now he asks you to whistle up your daring.

The dead man thinks there is enough in the dumpsters to feed
      an army.

The dead man hears the senators in the cloak room.

To the dead man, their language is flame retardant, their speeches
      are the cracking under the ice.

The dead man will turn the page if you will.

The dead man will lie prone to see into the abyss if you are
      beside him.

The dead man does not dare to say how happy he was.

It was the daredevil moment, when he decided.

He dared, he chose, he spun round, and in time the ground settled.

Here he stands, the dead man in his composure, but do you dare?

THE BOOK OF THE DEAD MAN (DECOMPOSITION)

Live as if you were already dead.

1. About the Dead Man and Decomposition

The dead man has a mulberry bush on the brain.

A mulberry chopped down thirty years ago, not one others can see.

It grew by the house, it was immediate, it was personal.

The dead man is of more than one mind about it.

The dead man's nature, like his brain, has been etched, chiseled,
      planed and diverted by a single bush, tree or flower, by a
      moment as quick as the claw foot of a bird overhead.

It takes little to inscribe in the dead man the forefront of
      the mystery.

To the dead man, that one mulberry was more than a forest.

To the dead man, the heron in his cedar was more than a rookery.

The dead man evades the notion of species to count by ones.

He is himself a species unlike others.

Others may sense, perceiving the dead man, that the silences
      of nature are a welcoming, and the sounds of nature
      are cautionary.

The dead man's love of nature, like yours, must be cognizant of
      the end.

It was not nature invented time.

It was not the devotees of entropy who said to live and let live.

The nature of nature will not be replicated in poetry ink.

The dead man greets Aristotle in the mindscape of imitation, it is
      not re-creation but a new world.

Such is nature to the dead man that the world may be endlessly
      reborn.

Even as the long dead live on in the dead man, so a mulberry bush
      may stay behind.

2. More About the Dead Man and Decomposition

Have you been waiting for the dead man to compose or
     to decompose?
The dead man, in becoming, unwrites and unsays.
The dead man has left no tracks in the loess, not in the humus, the
     loam, the dust, the salt or the talcum.
Not in the peat or chalk, the silt, the gravel or the spilled feed.
His footfalls in rain and snow lifted off, into the ethereal.
The dead man's weight is not dead weight but disperses, aerated
     and released.
Your memory of the dead man is a child's balloon, and where is
     that off to?
Of the dead man, still there remains the whole of nature.
In the whole of nature, the dead man is of many forms, a thread, a
     mesh, a graft, a skin, and the spine of the natural.
The dead man does not save for posterity, he dispenses with
     drafts, he lightens the future for his children.
He is out ahead of literature in this regard.
It was the *what* beyond words that made him speak to you this way.
Take a line from it when anxious, for it will compose you.
You may remember it, you may memorize it, you may take it to
     heart, it will endure in the interstices of time.
For here the excerpt is a whole, and the whole is an excerpt — it
     is so.

THE BOOK OF THE DEAD MAN (DRUGS)

Live as if you were already dead.

1. About the Dead Man and Drugs

The dead man tried to read the small type, but it was too small.

He tried to listen fast when the pitchman covered the side effects.

There was little to do but risk it.

It was the new drug for everything, a panacea.

He would no longer prowl the beaches looking for a word in
        a bottle.

He would not need to decipher the markings of crab shells, tea
        leaves, coffee grounds, the crystals or the clouds.

There would be no meaning of life, just life.

Then, in time, the dead man would feel a pain that had no name.

The side effects were death after one dose, muscle atrophy after
        two, kidney failure after three, there was a list.

The dead man has been on his knees, looking for a pill that rolled
        off the counter.

He has counted out dosages, placed the vials at bedside, woken
        himself in time, stayed up for the last, all that.

He knows that each pill is a concoction, like a cake, eat it all.

Each has its own way of defining a life.

So the dead man favors placebos.

As for body parts, he prefers to use the ones that hurt.

2. More About the Dead Man and Drugs

It hurts to stand up, so what?
It hurts uphill and downhill, as it should.
The dead man caught the general apathy toward the sociopolitical
      but dispelled it through better chemistry.
He thought hard, the way a high-jumper pictures his approach
      and his clearing of the bar before starting.
The dead man's foreshadowing can make something happen.
So he saw himself on a road away from the battlefield.
It is true, he could turn imagining into ability—the power to walk,
      say, first pictured, then realized.
The dead man is too corporeal for hallucinogens.
His drug is late nights, his obsession is now and its aftermath.
The dead man's drugs are not remedies but food for the overtimes.
They would be cure-alls, magical, miraculous, were they not dated.
The doc's charts show when time will run out, but it's a guess.
When the dead man is told he cannot walk, he walks.
He laughs at pain, he has a lot to learn.
The dead man is a geezer, and he is happy to hurt.

THE BOOK OF THE DEAD MAN (FAITH)

Live as if you were already dead.

1. About the Dead Man and Faith

The pathway drooped on which the dead man walked.

It snaked, it undulated, it thinned out like molten glass on the
blower's pipe.

In some circles, Vesuvius was thought a twist on the notion of fate,
a wrinkle in the measurement of an Edenic Fall.

The dead man smiled and watched.

He read about the saints, thinking he could do good.

He studied rituals, thinking he might take this or that plunge.

He investigated the super-realistic and unreal paintings in
Roman churches.

The pained Caravaggios, the hosts of madonnas and infants, the
star-crossed disciples.

How many sought to escape the flesh.

The artists put gold in the sky, they pierced their subjects until
they bled.

2. More About the Dead Man and Faith

The painters wrinkled robes and curtains in their art for effect.
They lashed the sea, they added thorns to the foliage.
They assembled crowds of believers clad in rags.
The dead man noted the rough grain of their faith.
He took stock of the commissions that fueled the glorifying.
In the dark chapels where a coin lit the art, there was also the
      dank history of laborers.
Thus the dead man inflicted disbelief on the framed narratives.
Outside, bits of pigeon soot bleached the walls.
There was a poster of a rock band, to appear in the near future.
Their faces mirrored and crowned the dead man's doubt.

THE BOOK OF THE DEAD MAN (FOOD)

Live as if you were already dead.

1. About the Dead Man and Food

The dead man likes chocolate, dark chocolate.

The dead man remembers custard as it was, spumoni as it was, shave ice as it was.

The dead man talks food with an active tongue, licks his fingers, takes seconds, but has moved on to salads.

It's the cheese, it's the crunch of the crunchy, it's the vinegar in the oil that makes a salad more than grass.

The dead man has a grassy disposition but no cow stomach for flappy leaves and diced croutons.

The dead man remembers oysterettes as they were.

He recalls good water and metal-free fish.

Headlights from the dock drew in blue claw crabs by the bucketful.

A flashlight showed them where the net lay.

If they looked bigger in the water than in the pail, they grew back on the stove.

It was like that, before salads.

The dead man, at the age he is, has redefined mealtime.

It being the quantum fact that the dead man does not believe in time, but in mealtime.

2. More About the Dead Man and Food

The dead man's happiness may seem unseemly.

By land or by sea, aloft or alit, happiness befalls us.

Were mankind less transfixed by its own importance, it would be
    harder to be happy.

Were the poets less obsessed with the illusion of the self, it would
    be more difficult to sing.

It would be crisscross, it would be askew, it would be zigzag,
        it would be awry, it would be cockeyed in any context
        of thought.

The dead man has felt the sensation of living.

He has felt the orgasmic, the restful, the ambiguous, the nearly-
        falling-over, the equilibrium, the lightning-in-the-bottle
        and the bottle in shards.

You cannot make the dead man write what you want.

The dead man offers quick approval but seeks none in return.

Chocolate is the more existential, it has the requisite absurdity, it
        loosens the gland.

The dead man must choose what he ingests, it cannot be anything
        goes in the world the world made.

So we come back to chocolate, which frees the dead man's tongue.

The dead man is every emotion at once, every heartbreak, every
        falling-down laugh riot, every fishhook that caught a finger.

THE BOOK OF THE DEAD MAN (FOUNDRY)

Live as if you were already dead.

1. About the Dead Man and the Foundry

The dead man hath founded the dead man's foundry.

He acted in the past perfect, he funded it with clean dirt, pure
     water and the spotless air.

Then he was melted, he was molded, he was poured and shook out.

He was ground and sanded, he was machined to a sweet tolerance.

The dead man took pains to stay alive, this was how.

It was the undersong of the self, the subtext, the no-man's-land's
     calling.

For the dead man was subterranean to start.

He was the tuber in the sun, the worm warming, the root that
     stays put.

The dead man became again what he was, he germinated.

It was the foundry of the sun, the foundry of the earth's core, the
     foundry of the electric light and the dry cell.

It was the retrofit energy that did it, the assemblage after
     dispersion, the kick in the pants we call chaos.

We are the children of a hothouse, among orchids that grow in lava.

2. More About the Dead Man and the Foundry

The foundry of the dead man pops and smolders with re-creation.

It is re-created in the titanic and the miniature, every detail.

Within the dead man, the same fire burns.

The same furnace, the same raw materials that made flesh.

The same red water, the same liquid sinew cooling.

The dead man's foundry has made weapons and plowshares, and
       those who use them.

The foundry and the forge, the shapes imprisoned in the molten
       streams of rough matter, these are precursors of the
       human, too.

The steam escaping from a wounded body is the foundry.

The heat of exhalation, the blush of desire, the red sun under the
       skin — they are the foundry.

And the high temperature of the ill, and the heat of the first
       foundry reassembling at its source.

If you believe in the reformation of energy, then you believe as
       well in the dead man.

He is heating up, and what is emotion?

THE BOOK OF THE DEAD MAN (FUNGI)

Live as if you were already dead.

1. About the Dead Man and Fungi

The dead man has changed his mind about moss and mold.

About mildew and yeast.

About rust and smut, about soot and ash.

Whereas once he turned from the sour and the decomposed, now
       he breathes deeply in the underbelly of the earth.

Of mushrooms, baker's yeast, fungi of wood decay, and the dogs
       preceding their masters to the burnt acre of morels.

And the little seasonals themselves, stuck on their wobbly
       pin stems.

For in the pan they float without crisping.

For they are not without a hint of the sublime, nor the curl of
       a hand.

These are the caps and hairdos, the mini-umbrellas, the zeppelins
       of a world in which human beings are heavy-footed
       mammoths.

Puffballs and saucers, recurrent, recumbent, they fill the
       encyclopedia.

Not wrought for the pressed eternity of flowers or butterflies.

Loners and armies alike appearing overnight at the point of return.

They live fast, they die young, they will be back.

2. More About the Dead Man and Fungi

Fruit of the fungi, a mushroom's birthing is an arrow from below.

It is because of Zeno's paradox that one cannot get there by
half-measures.

It is the fault of having anything else to do.

The dead man prefers the mushroom of the gatherer to that of
the farmer.

Gilled or ungilled, stemmed or stemless, woody or leathery, the
mushroom is secretive, yes, by nature.

Each mushroom was a button, each a flowering, some glow in
the dark.

Medicinal or toxic, each was lopped from the stump of eternity.

The dead man has seen them take the shapes of cups and saucers,
of sponges, logs and bird nests.

The dead man probes the shadows, he fingers the crannies and
undersides, he spots the mushroom underfoot just in time.

When the dead man saw a mushrooming cloud above Hiroshima,
he knew.

He saw that death was beautiful from afar.

He saw that nature is equidistant from the nourishing and the
poisonous, the good and the bad, the beginning and the end.

He knew the littlest mushroom, shivering on its first day, was
a signal.

THE BOOK OF THE DEAD MAN (HIS HATS)

Live as if you were already dead.

1. About the Dead Man and His Hats

The dead man has the face for wearing hats.
He has the hair for hats, the ears and eyebrows, the wrinkly
      forehead, the graying temples, a chameleon ability to fit in.
He has a way with the peaks of caps to be worn on rivers, on a
      prow seesawing toward the sun.
Even when, at the end, the deserts are turning to salt.
Even without a shirt or shoes — he will have a hat.
He has a talent for finding a scorpion in his boot, or in a hat on
      a chair.
He has a talent for stringing together what others think ashes.
He has crawled the field in a helmet, he has stood in the corner in
      a dunce cap, he was bar mitzvahed in a yarmulke.
He has danced round Astaire's top hat where it caps the Fred &
      Ginger edifice in Prague, it was hollow, it was lofty.
He has walked Havana, Managua, Belgrade in contentious times,
      incognito, private in a hat.
He has a method for shading his eyes, call it a knack.
He wears his cap backward to run with a kite by the sea.
His favorite is a feed hat, a crumpled plasterer's cap that touts
      what farm animals eat.

54

2. More About the Dead Man and His Hats

Winters, in a watch cap, he sits at the café, a philosopher wrapped
      in an odor of strong coffee.
The dead man can wear any hat, that of Pan or Dionysus and also
      of that dour fellow, Chaos.
To the surrealist inside him, the moon is a mothball in a closet
      of fedoras.
To the realist in him, a covered head is how you get away when you
      find yourself on the target.
To the futurist in him, the dead man's hat is what's to come, he can
      just make it out if he pulls down the peak and squints.
To the cynic and soldier, naturally, every hat is a helmet.
His beret has a built-in tilt, and his hard hat a dent.
The dead man does not come to you hat in hand.
He has a hatful of thoughts he never mentions, nor does he spit on
      the plate when invited for dinner.
Like you, the dead man has kept a lot under his hat, and still will.
The dead man is neither a youngster nor a show-off.
He is the architect of an underground hat culture.
He wears a hat because he can't be taking the time to comb
      his hair.

THE BOOK OF THE DEAD MAN (HIS HEALTH)

Live as if you were already dead.

1. About the Dead Man's Health

At least one exotic plant — an orchid, say.

At least one uncommon mineral — chromium, perhaps.

Bandages, tourniquets, splints, casts, wraps and salves.

The dead man continues patching where he can, covering the
damage, propping the skeleton, reinforcing the shell,
repairing, reinventing.

Here he is in the archway, hesitant in the corridor to the doctors.

There he is at the rooftop balustrade, his coat open, proclaiming
unintelligibly while the white coats urge him down.

His health is but a distraction.

He finds himself again and again in the amphitheaters of
the obstinate.

How to prove his sentences are philosophical gadgets, stand-ins
for numerals from another plane, standards for animal
behavior?

The dead man hears the selfish ones refusing to feel.

Their millions are increasing, whose skin cannot breathe.

The dead man carries water to the tar paper shacks.

He tells the poor the way to the nation's Capitol, they should know.

2. More About the Dead Man's Health

The dead man's *zero amount* is your *never ever.*

His treatments of the body politic require roses bearing thorns.

His remedies for innocence need water and wood.

The dead man and the dead woman have had words with our
       senators.

The dead man is not up to refusing you health care, he is different.

Have you heard about the dead man in pajamas, his months
       in bed?

He was given a long claw for picking up things, it was his toy.

His legs were as thickly wrapped as a panda's, comical, ungainly,
       diminished.

To be undiminished is the dead man's goal for health care.

Universal care belies a fixed number for those who raise
       its standard.

So the dead man's medicine is not a gel to make things shine.

It is gristle and bone, heart and soul, and spit for polish.

The dead man cups an ear to listen for the healing.

THE BOOK OF THE DEAD MAN (HIS OLDE ODE)

Live as if you were already dead.

1. About the Dead Man's Olde Ode

The dead man has been writing the oldster's olde ode.

His oldest ode was the beautiful song, the sound of living at all.

Now ye olde ode is also the news.

Even if there were times when the horizon arced over the planet
too acutely to reveal the others.

Even if the dead man could not turn enough to see them.

And if the keening of mourners was daily to be pulverized by the
sound of motors departing.

Yet the engine of the planet purred, and the wheel sang.

So it was the nature of all and everything that absorbed the
dead man.

The world was full of nameless things that words could not keep.

Some wanted the dead man to disown the silence, and he
considered it.

He had heard how scary the silence could be.

He knew that an ode to joy had to be thumpingly hearable and
make the floorboards bounce.

The dead man knew, also, that things end.

His hope was that he be free in the glare of truth to bask in the
warm-up to the furnace.

And of course to dance.

That he might celebrate before the impact, that he might sing the
approach of the parasites.

A vase may lie for what we think forever in fragments, but a dead
man may not be reassembled.

You see that it is well that the dead man has to take a break now
and then.
A respite from the olde ode that was, like every pleasure, an
escape from time.
The illusions of art have been to the dead man both beautiful
and tiring.
The dead man adjusts the piano bench, he resets the reed, he tunes
the drum and marimba, he turns the pegs at fret's end.
The dead man cannot resist the music of the spheres.

2. More About the Dead Man's Olde Ode

We're back, the self and the other self, the dead man alive and the
      other one looking ahead.

Were you anticipating some hully-gully, some hooey, some
      hanky-panky?

The dead man has had to forgo certain pleasures because of
      the war.

If you ask which war, take your pick or wait for it.

War is the newsy part of the ode, part of the olde ode and part of
      the new.

The dead man has been increasingly absorbed by elsewhere and
      others, he is one of them.

The body politic suffered, but the missing arms and legs did not
      stop him.

Even the cruelest head wounds could not stop the dead man
      from thinking.

So the dead man apologizes for appearing to celebrate wartime, for
      he does not.

It was inescapable that pleasure kept on throughout and between
      the wars, and there were many.

The wars were as constant as lawnmowers in the cemeteries.

In time, the dead man no longer pushed the life force into the face
      of death.

He had become the first patient, he had perfected the wait-and-see.

He had learned, he had looked it up, he had lived through.

The dead man listens for the sounds of involuntary joy.

He hears the treaties shrivel while children laugh in the yard.

He feels the tremor underneath the long lines of laborers and
       follows the weary to the tavern after work.

So long as there can be a few last drops, the dregs, the bottom of
       the barrel, a sip, a taste, a bite, a sniff of the apple, for that
       long can time-to-come retain its welcome.

The dead man's ode was always about the planet and the dance.

It was always about the collapse of empires.

It was always about the silvery cloud edge that winked as it
       reshaped itself.

He who would last awhile must sprinkle himself widely among all
       that is not himself, you odists listen.

THE BOOK OF THE DEAD MAN (*KISS KISS*)

Live as if you were already dead.

1. About the Dead Man (*Kiss Kiss*)

The dead man is of the future, but he will not breathe a word of it.

The dead man will say he is the patchwork offspring of Mother
Nature and Father Time.

He frames it thus when folksy, as others say *tsk tsk* to youth or *kiss
kiss* for goodbye.

He is common, even so he has tried to pry official fingers from the
nuclear button.

He is common, even so he has tried to smoke out the cranks.

The dead man has seen his nation shoot itself in the foot with a
blood lust for guns.

He has seen it smoke itself to death.

He has lived among the wistful who can only rub a brass lamp.

He has boarded with the fry cook and the pool tender, the
taskmaster and the idler.

He doesn't wear a suit, he is small-town, common, he is one-at-
a-time.

2. More About the Dead Man (*Kiss Kiss*)

Where now a cyclotron spirals particles at Brookhaven National
      Laboratory, there was Camp Upton.
The dead man saw the soldiers mustering out.
He was a child among the khaki strap undershirts, buffeted by the
      commotion at the edge of imminent release.
This was the old way of war, one tour of duty and a discharge.
The dead man's father drove to the camp to hire a veteran.
And there were prisoners, then, working at roadsides or in fields,
      happy to have been pulled from the fighting.
And the veterans of older wars who said nothing afterward.
The dead man is a veteran of an army rent by the hubris of empire.
Now dead men and dead women live among the bereaved of war,
      live and pass away, live and pass away.
The dead man dies with the fallen soldier and the aged veteran
      equally.

THE BOOK OF THE DEAD MAN (LIGHT SKELETON)

Live as if you were already dead.

1. About the Dead Man and the Light Skeleton

What if the dead man were a skeleton with wings?

Black and white, an inflatable skin without blood, no gristle, no
      spiky relays, no stretchy tendons.

Picture him having shed his inner organs.

He is light now, he can hover, he can temper your fear with a sense
      of floating.

There is, on the one hand, a bucket of heavy innards, and on the
      other, there is the unexpected lightness of the dead man.

He enters in a whiteness more white than white, a doorway to
      the sun.

Only look up to see him.

It seems he entered your consciousness without tripping the alarm.

He moved past the watchdogs, who remain silent.

It is a whiteness more white than a cessation of thought.

2. More About the Dead Man and the Light Skeleton

The butterfly was too small, the hummingbird too quick, the
      nightingale too rare, it took the dead man.
It was a blinding light, a white glass to the past, a life in midair.
From the sun spreading, from cinders flying, from the whistle of
      skeleton bones, the dead man may enter.
As from a line of gull song screaming, he may suddenly beach.
From a ripple back of the bricks, from a wisp on high, from the
      poppies puckering, from unwavering resolve, he may
      be born.
What if he comes bearing the rib cage of starvation and a cape?
He may enter as an irrational surge of current.
He may be too large for the space allotted him, and take the air.
He may be the parade balloon you hoped had escaped.
The dead man adds bounce to the hours, and he stays up.

THE BOOK OF THE DEAD MAN (THE METRONOME)

Live as if you were already dead.

1. About the Dead Man and the Metronome

The dead man's straight shot is a jagged path from the surface, a
    sawtooth descent, a switchback of expectations.
They will be making lemonade out of lemons, or so they say.
They will ululate as the dead man passes, they will hurry at a good
    clip behind the body, they may rattle their bracelets and
    key rings.
They do this after each assassination, too.
For now, the dead man has merely closed the metronome, folded
    the triangle and unwound the clock.
The dead man, as an insider, thought like an outsider.
He is a kind of Klein bottle, a sort of human Möbius strip.
He was not schooled in beauty.
He was not swaddled in entitlement or posh classrooms.
He just had a tic for looking around the corner like the
    double-jointed fans of superheroes.
Of course he has the powers of prescience and prophecy,
    who doesn't?
He saw early that space eats time, and he moved to the periphery.
The dead man is a fringe element.

2. More About the Dead Man and the Metronome

The dead man quit the jamboree at the point of congestion.
He could not see from far inside the populace.
He avoided the group singing, the book lists, his own first opinions.
He made light of the flap over who matters and what counts.
He will leave in his wake a budding new music hovering in synapses.
The dead man's metronome is irregular, the regular one
        was remedial.
He doubles the stresses of, "Give me your tired, your poor."
Because his government has stopped listening.
The elected took piano lessons, they learned to count, they tapped
        their feet.
Then they took down a nation by the numbers.
The dead man thinks our minorities will save us from them.
Where there are too many of them, there are too few of us.
The dead man hears in the metronome the sound of hubris.
The dead man proclaims an elastic measure only some can follow.

THE BOOK OF THE DEAD MAN
(MOUNT RUSHMORE)

Washington, Jefferson, T. Roosevelt, Lincoln

Live as if you were already dead.

1. About the Dead Man and Mount Rushmore

To become the face of a mountain—you'd think he'd want it.

To be the high cheekbones on high, the forehead that bedevils the
crowd with its facade of knowing.

But the dead man hears the crowing of the birds, who alight
without a semblance of symbolism or accolades.

Yet if the dead man should lie prone, he, too, may be lifted over
eons to a peak.

He, too, may be thrust into the heavens.

If, that is, he is not slowly lowered into the simmering core of a
mountain-making workshop.

Let him look now at the great faces being groomed by weather.

Let him climb hand-over-hand with a toothpick in his mouth and
a cap jaunty for the thrill.

No president shall fall from this perch, he thinks.

The dead man would like to bring back the earthly versions of
these four.

To set them at the doors to the latest presidential libraries with
torches in their hands.

To coat the war criminals with the slime of their origins, to spit
boulders at the Congress.

It is, the dead man thinks, a long way down from these four.

Their faces were lifted, who would never have sanctioned a
face-lift.

Their visages were blasted clean, who were men with dirt under
their nails.

Their sixty-foot heads went on whispering beneath the shroud
placed by John Fire Lame Deer of the Lakota.

They went on whispering, the dead man could hear it, they
debated what is necessary, what is inescapable, what is
random and what can be forgiven.

The dead man can hear atonements so slight they only bend the
fire reeds in wind.

He can sense apologies so tentative they murmur only when the
brook runs.

2. More About the Dead Man and Mount Rushmore

To the argument over who was anyplace first, the dead man
        offers himself.
For he is made of particles that came from the near and far, from
        the creek bed and the seven wonders of the ancient world.
The dead man knows the quantum means that you cannot fix him.
So here, he thinks, is the visible difference.
Here on this Rushmore is the chiseled perpetuity to which
        mankind looks up.
Yet the dead man is of another stripe, another streak, another
        vein, another lode and deposit, not to be recovered in toto.
You'd think he'd want it, to be of the earth itself, but of course he
        will be.
Without his wanting to.
There will be another tectonic uplifting, count on it.
The dead man can feel a spasm so deep it is recorded only when a
        needle shudders on graph paper.
Here come, reborn, the stone Cheyenne and the stone Lakota.
Here come the displaced, here come the rabble.
The dead man is in the way, here come the warriors on horseback.
The dead man knows that the victorious will win by any means.
He can hear the long rue, he can hear the late regret, he can hear
        the apologies so undermined by monuments that they
        surface out of reach.
They are in the air, they are weightless, they are shadows the sun
        permits when it chooses.

Up he goes with wonderment and a loose tooth.
Up he goes with sore knees and a locked trigger finger.
Up he goes without piety where the stone-faced have been
    sentenced to look straight ahead.

THE BOOK OF THE DEAD MAN (MOVIE THEATER)

Live as if you were already dead.

1. About the Dead Man and the Movie Theater

The dead man has been reading subtitles in the dark.

They leave out some anatomy, they cut the cussing.

He looks up and down to see the figures on the screen, who are
>   larger than their words.

He tries to follow the players as they persist in their visions.

One of them wants to go straight, another seeks revenge.

The dead man has seen too much, now he hopes the lovers
>   don't fight.

Likewise, he prefers those who are still coming of age to get there.

The dead man thinks their speech contains the seeds of
>   its destruction.

The cold subtitles mute their passions.

The scene morphs, the light shifts, the seats creak, all of it safely.

2. More About the Dead Man and the Movie Theater

The dead man returns to the dark magic of the movie theater.
A sensitivity to light blankets the room as the house lamps dim.
The red Exit signs slide further into the dead man's
        peripheral vision.
From high up, the projector sends a tide of light overhead, a river
        of slivers that reassemble at the silver screen.
Now the dead man is emptied of foreknowledge.
The film begins, there may be foreshadowing, flashback, time shifts.
The theater swells with points of view.
Let him last through the credits at the end, blinking as he wakes.
To the dead man, every movie is a home movie he is privy to.
He is the eye behind the camera, he is a mystery to the characters.
They are not themselves, they pretend he cannot see them.

THE BOOK OF THE DEAD MAN (THE NORTHWEST)

Live as if you were already dead.

And the fish swim in the lake
and do not even own clothing.
EZRA POUND, "SALUTATION"

1. About the Dead Man and the Northwest

Picture the dead man in two rooms in the northwest corner of
      his being.
In the one, it is day, and in the other, night, and he lives in both.
His street dead-ends at a cliff above a rattling of ropes clanging
      on masts and the whimper of lazy tides.
There are lumps on the sea bottom.
There is also, as elsewhere, a worldly stomping that threatens the
      scale pan of justice.
The dead man fingers a lucky stone like Casanova his
      address book.
For the Northwest, which may feel ashen to the displaced
      Easterner under the white of a winter sky, pleases him greatly.
It is the density of forest that overwhelms his language, as the
      dexterity of the tides smooths his hours and the mountain
      passes frame the light at midday.
The dead man smells the faint fizz of froth at shore's edge.
It is the smell of the soap the adolescent rinses away before a date.
It is the loamy feel in his throat when a young man is asked
      to speak.
The dead man has opened the map, and run his finger along the
      interstates, and driven west to land's edge.
The dead man's distant friends look toward England, it is old.
The dead man is himself old but is forever newly at home.

He who grew up near the sunrise feels more at home near
the sunset.
That's the dead man's duality, drawn east-to-west and
south-to-north.

2. More About the Dead Man and the Northwest

Though we make a junkyard of the sea, still the fish wink.
The dead man's turf is piled with lug nuts and vinyl, tubing
       and wire, razor blades, batteries, bubble wrap and book
       bags — name anything.
Still the dead man toasts both the present and the absence to come.
Salmon that went against the current.
Madrones that peeled without a whimper, you seers take notice.
The dead man has a favorite heron because they see one
       another daily.
And the one sits in the other's tree and squawks when it flies off
       or returns.
What makes one go here or there, and stay, may be the rhythm of
       the heart, or the firing of brain cells or the feel of the air.
The dead man has heavy bones, he does not float.
He has small pores.
He cannot be smelled as quickly by the wolf, a trait that brought
       them face to face.
He walks by the elk and the deer who do not care.
Like them, he knows time by the look of the light and the smell.
The dead man, standing between the Pacific and Cascades, at the
       tip of the Quimper Peninsula, is almost out of time.
The dead man is not as much about *doing*.
The dead man was, and will be, and, for now, just is.

THE BOOK OF THE DEAD MAN (NOTHING)

Live as if you were already dead.

1. About the Dead Man and Nothing

The dead man knows nothing.

He is powerless to stop the battles, he has no way to reattach the
    arms and legs.

He cannot stuff the fallen soldier's insides back inside.

He has no expertise in the matter of civilian corpses, nor of
    friendly fire, nor beheadings, nor revenge, nor suicide.

He does not know the depth of depth charges, or the exact
    pressure that detonates a land mine.

The dead man has given his all so that now, if he once knew, he
    knows nothing.

He is emptied, he is the resonant cavity of which he spoke when it
    was music he was thinking of.

Let him be now the leftover button of his work shirt.

Permit him his fading mirror, his sputtering circuits, his secrets,
    his tears, his noonday duels with the sun.

Let him ride the roads in the bucket of an earth mover, can it hurt?

Let him stand under the icicles, can he catch cold?

For the dead man is stagnant without knowledge, and he cannot
    survive the demise of philosophy or art.

To the dead man they were not spectacles, but survival skills.

To the dead man, the world was but a birthmark that befell
    original space.

To say that the dead man knows nothing is to see him at the
    beginning, who can it hurt?

Before all this, he was nothing.

2. More About the Dead Man and Nothing

Don't bet he won't be born.

Before all this, this that is so much, he was not himself.

He was the free heat of space and then the salt of the earth.

He was the ring around the moon, foretelling.

The dead man had no station when he came to be, just a strange
      nakedness in the light.

He did not know what he was to do, this was before clocks.

So he decided to stab the dirt, to tumble in happiness and writhe
      in pain, and to flap his way into space.

To go home.

It was a swell idea for the dead man, and he pinned it to his chest.

Give him that, that he crystallized a plan, that he made from
      smoke something to him as real as quartz, ivory, or the hoof
      of a gelding.

The dead man had the whole world to transform or perfect
      or outlive.

He wrote the book of nothing and no-time that entombed all time
      and all that took place in time.

The dead man could not be hammered by analysis.

Let him horn in on your fury, whatever it was, and it will abate.

The energy that became form will disperse, never again to be what
      we were.

Look out the window to see him, no, the other one.

THE BOOK OF THE DEAD MAN
(THE NUCLEAR SUBMARINE)

Live as if you were already dead.

1. About the Dead Man and the Submarine

Earlier, the dead man fired the mortar and bazooka, lobbed the
grenade and swept the barrel of the automatic.

He boarded the troop copter, the armored carrier, the jeep.

He shouldered the rifle and wore the night revolver on duty.

He was called out when the AWOL soldier lay down on the
railroad track.

He kept his head down on the infiltration course.

He shared his foxhole, his rations, his canteen.

He was not brave, he was one of the boys, he would have gone
along if called.

Those dead man days shrink aboard the nuclear sub, touring its
armament, its math and physics, its dark genius.

It takes two grips to fix a bayonet but only fingers to launch an
atom bomb.

The dead man descended to the lower decks where the gauges
were masked.

2. More About the Dead Man and the Submarine

The crew moved quicker, not stepping but sliding down the
        vertical ladders with a whoosh.
The crew that slept on mattresses between the missiles.
The crew that worked in colored lamplight before a puzzle
        of gauges.
The crew that loses its depth of field to each six months at sea.
The crew members listening but never transmitting, their location
        the captain's secret.
And the torpedoes longer than a string of limos at the ready.
In the labyrinth below the waterline, a network of
        interdependence, call it a warren, a burrow, a den, a lair.
Call it reliance, call it trust, call it faith.
The dead man, like you, wants to be safe, but is not.
The dead man, like you, is in the sights, on the target, inside the
        zone, acceptably collateral, and a man on a mission.

THE BOOK OF THE DEAD MAN (THE NUMBERS)

Live as if you were already dead.

1. About the Dead Man and the Numbers

The dead man is outside the pale.

The dead man makes space for himself the way a soccer player
      moves to the place to be next.

The angles shift, the pace slows and picks up, it matters more,
      then less, then more, then less, and others run by in
      both directions.

One of them may slow to stoke the embers of a failing thought.

For example, the dead man restores the poet's ambition to plumb
      the nature of existence.

Sometimes he, sometimes she, asks the dead man what it is to live
      as if one were already dead.

It's the feel of an impression in the earth, a volume in space, an
      airy drift upward.

It's downwind and upwind at the same time.

It's a resonance to wrap one's mind around, like a bandage
      beneath which the healing may happen.

It's the idea of turf beyond the neighborhood.

It's a cold flame in a hot season.

It's what you do facing the guns.

2. More About the Dead Man and the Numbers

Here we go, with what it takes.

The dead man wakes in a dream, lungs aching as if the night were
      a stairway or a hill.

Is he indoors or out, an insider in public or an outsider at home?

He hears a splash of tissue in a knee and a click as his shoulder
      slips the edge of an obstruction.

You would think he thinks himself awake, but the dead man
      does not.

He has a way of making the ephemeral last, the rusting slow, the
      leaf hang, the bullet hold up in midair.

In the waking world, there are too many of us to tell, the ushers
      are overwhelmed by the numbers wanting a box seat.

The preacher offering a future world, the historian waxing
      nostalgic, and the dead man underwriting them is what
      it takes.

How is it to be the dead man among shifting loyalties?

It means living in the interstices, swimming in the wake of the big
      boats, crossing the borders on back roads.

It means taking the field with those whose lives are numbered.

It means finding space for when it will matter.

THE BOOK OF THE DEAD MAN (ORCHARDS)

Live as if you were already dead.

1. About the Dead Man and the Orchards

The dead man walks among apples and oranges.

He favors each in its time.

He has had, for some long time, little in common with the prudes
and prunes.

With the cross, flush-faced, trembly handed, antiplay, windy,
laced-up, unwild, odorous defenders of poetic retrograde.

Notwithstanding, let us yet honor the past and cotton to its
iambic civilities.

The dead man is a metrician in disguise and a wild man in a mask.

Let the hour come when he finds himself at the edge, and still he
will not satisfy your cravings for a talky why.

Or for toys.

His laughter, existential and absurdist, will linger for you when
the little billy club jokes have gone their way.

You see a bowl of fruit on a table and think what?

An invitation to make art?

Or do you see again, as does the dead man, your father picking
fruit for pennies — if he told you.

When the dead man was barely a child, he remembered that he
did not try to remember.

The white porcelain of the boys' urinal was to him an early
blank page.

This is true, he does not recall his childhood but for the feelings.

He was not afraid, he was sometimes afraid, he was always afraid.

In his father's house there were many rooms, and places under the
     beds, and room in the closets, and an attic like a kerchief
     over it all.
The dead man took survival training without leaving home.

2. More About the Dead Man and the Orchards

The dead man prolongs the memory of an immigrant father.
He recalls a father who ran the trenches to drag off the dead, it was
      the old country, it was long ago.
That is why he is the dead man, that and the future.
The dead man remembers, too, the eleven horses cresting the hill as
      he walked toward them through the buffalo sod.
That memory is his own, he didn't make it up, it apes the recent past.
From such outings does pleasure pleasure, as a bite of a wild apple
      may open the day.
To the dead man, the planet is an orchard of the whole.
He seeks the play of fruit scent in the wind, he edges by the hour
      toward the earth that trembles but is not afraid.
The dead man wrote in an age of handmade lace which passed for
      an artifact of true nature.
He wrote in a time of inverted bowls, of minds unable to bear the
      cross but wept the red tears of the guilty survivor.
He heard them say, "hot damn," "cool cat."
He stayed up late to sing and dance – alone.
Nothing better embodies the human condition than the dead man.
He has the fermentation on his skin, the same.
He is the picker, he is the accountant, he weighs the baskets.
It was a good thing there were horses.
They let his father ride at night too far for the guards to see
      him gone.
It was the orchard that fed him, now it is the dead man who
      nourishes the orchard for next time.

THE BOOK OF THE DEAD MAN (THE PALM)

Live as if you were already dead.

1. About the Dead Man and the Fortune-Telling Palm

The dead man lives with omens, tentative forecasts, strict
    calculations, guesses and earnest prophecies.
Also, estimations, conjectures, projections, the weight of statistics
    and the drift of hope.
Those who know the dead man are beside themselves with
    contradictions, what to say and from which self?
For he is here and not here, as it will be foretold after he has gone.
There was the famous cat in a box, and the quantum cat, which is
    a way of looking at the cat without seeing it.
It is not enough that space is curved, even a fly's eyes see only
    a little.
Now comes the panorama of the lifeline, the health line, the head
    line and fate.
It isn't easy, and he drinks coffee.
It isn't easy, and his fingers hurt from striking the keys.
It isn't a snap, and his wrists crackle when he waves or beckons.

2. More About the Dead Man and the Fortune-Telling Palm

In the second act of the play, the statues decided to work.

They stepped off their pedestals to become like us, common hands.

The dead man's hands fit the crown of his head.

They can cup a knee or cover his ears or muffle his speech.

Go to the fortune-teller with your hands behind your back.

Go to the wise man with an empty mind.

Holding up his hands in front of his eyes, the dead man sees the
      mounts of Venus and Luna.

He sees himself holding love and the night, and his fate is in his
      hands, too.

He wills himself to flatten his hands, one against the other, it
      isn't easy.

It isn't easy, and he doesn't pray.

ᴚOOK OF THE DEAD MAN (THE PAUSE)

Live as if you were already dead.

Marcelo Lucero, b. 1971–d. Nov. 8, 2008
Patchogue, New York

1. About the Dead Man and the Pause

Seven young men went looking to beat up a Hispanic and found
      one and killed him, and the dead man will speak of it.
The dead man pauses to consider, to ruminate, to extrapolate, to
      ponder, to chew over, to digest.
He knows they wanted to stop the world, who fell in warfare.
He knows they wanted to stop time, who faced the guns.
The seven who stabbed to death a stranger wanted to stop their
      anger but could not.
The dead man has to be a dead man to make it stop.
He has to take stock, which takes time, time that is ravaged
      by entropy.
The dead man has invented God.
God is the filling-in of the blanks, the filling-up of the cavities and
      wounds, the words that blanket the cold, the eyes looking,
      the body expectant, the one chance in a million.
The dead man has also invented the inner life.
The inner life is the re-creation of the young Ecuadorian knifed
      to death in Patchogue just days before the invention of the
      inner life.
The inner life is the rebirth of the young Marine sharpshooter
      who a week earlier was memorialized by renaming a bridge.
The inner life, the inner life... is no escape.

So the dead man has invented the pause, which is God, which is
    the inner life.
Such small particles may float free from any action that a dead
    man may die again, or live again, seen only by the few who
    pause to consider.
It was the dead man who said that the purpose of life was to look
    out the window.
What window, what perch, what time, what self?
The dead man is halfway up the ladder, or is coming down.
The dead man has less self than the newsworthy, less ego than the
    sophisticate, less purchase than the wealthy.
The dead man will not sell his secrets, nor tattle.
Many others must know before the dead man will admit that he
    knows, too.

2. More About the Dead Man and the Pause

The dead man abides in the pauses, in the gaps, the interstices, the
 breaches, the slits, the fissures, the chasms, the in-betweens
 and not-yets.
Picture a clock one can reach to turn back the hands.
Picture a handkerchief not yet folded.
The dead man opens again the wound of the victim.
When the dead man, kneeling by the body, tries to stand, he
 becomes nauseated.
Because the dead man is you, was always you, he tallies the crimes
 you know from the papers, they are local.
Here is the slaying of last week, and the one from last night, and
 the map of neighborhoods coded for killings.
The dead man set out to speak of the one crime, the one whose
 face is on page 1.
The dead man tore the seven bullies in half, he could not resist.
He kept alive the picture of the slain, while he crumpled the
 defense lawyers who have no case but their fees.
Such nice haircuts, such well-fit new suits, and the defendants sit
 still, too.
If they choose not to testify, well, the dead man will use their
 silence against them.
The dead man wanted to write poetry, but the streets were blocked.
The way forward was too loud, too fraught, it was a rebuke to the
 applications of beauty.
The dead man can't see straight, it's you again.

The dead man wanted to write about it, but police tape kept
     him away.
The dead man is leaving it to you, what are you going to do?
If the sun came out, if the handkerchief remained in the hip
     pocket, if the clock was on time, if the fire siren only
     meant lunch, if the ambulance did not have to drive on the
     shoulder, if the fatalities ran down to zero, the dead man
     would be comical.
The dead man has heard the jokes about Saint Peter.
The dead man invented God, he invented the inner life, they
     were easy.
Heaven is harder.

Live as if you were already dead.

1. About the Dead Man in Peacetime, If and When

If and when the war is over, the dead man's days will seem longer.

When the ammo is spent, the funds discharged, when the fields have
   shut down and the flares fallen, an hour will take an hour.

Time for the dead man lengthens when the shooting stops.

The waiting for the next war to begin can seem endless, though it
   take but a week, a month or a year.

The low intensity conflicts, the raids and assassinations, the
   deployments and withdrawals, the coups and revolutions, the
   precursors and aftermaths — it's a lifetime of keeping track.

It's as if the sun fell and fizzled — somewhere.

Then the black, white and gray propaganda, the documents planted
   on corpses, the reading of tea leaves and bones…

The dead man takes stock in the darkness of peacetime.

The Judas goats stand waiting in the corrals.

We are the sheep that gambol through dreamless nights.

A quietude hangs in the air, an expectancy, the shimmer that some
   believe presages alien life forms.

The calm before the stampede.

It was wartime when love arrived, yes, love.

It was wartime when the virtuosi performed, standing on their heads,
   as it were, for peacetime is our upside-down time.

2. More About the Dead Man in Peacetime, If and When

On a field of armed conflict, in the midst of rushing water, at the
       lip of a canyon, by the border of a fire-torched desert, in
       the overdark of a rain forest, where else was there ever
       but here?

Do you think poetry is for the pretty?

Look up and down, then, avoiding the hillocks that hold the
       remains.

The dead man, too, sees the puffy good nature of the clouds.

He welcomes, too, the spring blooming that even the grass salutes.

The dead man has made peace with temporary residence and the
       eternal Diaspora.

Oh, to live in between, off the target, blipless on the radar, silent
       on the sonar.

To keep one's head down when the satellites swoop over.

Not even to know when the last war is reincarnated and the next
       one conceived.

The dead man sings of a romantic evening in the eerie flickering
       of the last candle.

He whistles, he dances, he writes on the air as the music passes.

It was in wartime that the dead man conceived sons.

The dead man lifts a glass to the beauties of ruin.

The dead man is rapt, he is enveloped, he is keen to be held.

THE BOOK OF THE DEAD MAN (PUZZLE)

Live as if you were already dead.

1. About the Dead Man and the Puzzle

In a fat chair by a window, with a mug of coffee, the dead man
      puzzles.

He who was asked where is beauty sits in its presence.

The color blue is beautiful to him, and the blues, and the black
      and white of a musical score.

The dead man dislikes the color red on politicians, though he likes
      red hair, red horses and red-blooded dissent.

It's a puzzle, what people like, and the dead man is dumbstruck to
      tally the voting.

The dead man trusts Occam's razor to shave the excess, but where
      is a barber fit to be president?

The dead man has seen governments take their star turns while
      the suffering continued backstage.

It is a puzzle at the window that the workers go forth as always.

It is a puzzle that the mugging continues.

He has seen the protesters baptized by water cannon and small
      arms fire.

He has seen the faces pressed against the gap-toothed gate of the
      presidential mansion.

He has seen the protesters thrash about at a distance and go home.

Beauty, then, is, where else, in the mind's eye, recollected
      in tranquillity.

So, in the autumn of the year 2008, beauty is a puzzle, just that.

Beauty is a helpless bias, is it not?

And the grape was beautiful that the dead man changed into water.

2. More About the Dead Man and the Puzzle

The dead man puzzles out the planetary system.

Caught in the political orbit, he assembles an aggregate of
minorities.

The dead man has fit together mankind's wish to do good with
mankind's wish to do well and the explosion of rampant
capitalism.

The dead man is a dinner guest with much on his plate.

Say it again, the dead man is dumbstruck.

Say it once more, the dead man is puzzled, all at sea, baffled but
not bamboozled.

The dead man works the green puzzles of the earth, the white
puzzles of the poles, the blue puzzles of the sky and oceans,
the orange puzzle of the setting sun, the yellow puzzle of
the pollen, the red puzzle of the bloodstream.

It has been the dead man's fate to know and yet be puzzled.

It has taken all this time to be startled.

Just as it has taken these years of entropy to be raised from
the living.

The dead man provokes no envy, for he has left you everything.

The dead man who peered from the gaps in the grape vines.

The dead man who spoke to the man-face in the moon.

He has mugged his way through the illusions of passage, winged
it among the interrogators, uttered the rash idea after
long thought.

He has honed and honed Occam's razor.

At the end, it was the unmiraculous mint that refreshed him where
he lay taking increasingly shallower breaths.

THE BOOK OF THE DEAD MAN (RADIO)

Live as if you were already dead.

1. About the Dead Man and Radio

How best might the dead man organize the signals from multiple
    receivers?
The dead man's pal has been out counting alien transmissions.
And many of his friends are awaiting the next life, whether soon
    or well down the reincarnation road.
The air is filled with oscillations.
The tuning fork at the center of the universe is fully aquiver.
The phenomenal is personal, ever more so.
The team was locked down in the hotel before the big game.
We have the clotheshorse, we have fitness, we have advertising, we
    have candy and infection.
We live with godsends and bad luck.
The dead man spots the pitfalls in perfection.
He has teammates down the field and farther out in space.
He has pacifist friends in the military and assassins in his Rolodex.
It's tricky to climb the ladder while wearing the tool belt.
It's human to think one knows where the portal is.
It's scientific to measure the infinite.
The dead man best expresses the alternating current, the
    modulations, the morphing and segues.
The dead man is syntax, the dead man is whole, the dead man's
    sentences last.
He hears the voices overlapping in the air, the signals folding into
    one another, the circumnavigational layering.
He listens to the call-in shows of the past.

He hears the pages crackling as the news of the day is rebroadcast.
A cacophony of harmonics and parasitics overlays the airwaves.
The dead man is happy among aliens and outsiders, he favors the
    party favors that make noise.

2. More About the Dead Man and Radio

After the long warm-up, the dead man mustered the stamina to
      begin again.
If you, reader, cannot take another step, the dead man
      understands.
If you want finality, one-piece art, a never changing document.
The dead man's portrait changes according to atmospheric
      pressure, and he has been known to grimace when others
      are laughing and laugh when others are earnest.
It was a corporate disadvantage not to fit in, but he lives elsewhere.
There was lingo on both sides of the beat oscillator, look it up.
There was meaning in the shrugs, the grunts and screams, the
      giggles and yelps.
Why not life as it is instead of these artifacts?
The dead man was shaped by radio, by ear, by temperature
      and static.
It was radio radiating and the phases of the moon.
The dead man is of the invisible world that is itself material.
Keep the little whistle in your pocket, it will be handy.
And a flashlight for the cemetery, the stones wear away.
When the flag flutters, when the tide slaps the shore, when the car
      tires send up a hum during rush hour, that's radio.
It was radio when the dead man's ears flared.
It was radio loosed the dead man's imagination.
It was the wire recorder, the single-track tape player, the
      homemade drums, it was sound waves that struck him.

Now the rooftops are antennas, the drainpipes resonate, the air is
    awash in signals, the dishes on the sides of homes will be
    collecting a flood of sound scraps.
The dead man learned to listen to the one among many.
Now the dead man is surrounded, blanketed, stirred-in to the
    seething stew of a universe of eternal radio.
For the dead man, as for you, some words are internal, try *milk,*
    try *dress,* try, for the dead man, *radio.*
First listen, then know.

THE BOOK OF THE DEAD MAN
(THE RED WHEELBARROW)

Live as if you were already dead.

1. About the Dead Man and "The Red Wheelbarrow"

The dead man has been asked about a red wheelbarrow.
Not an actual wheelbarrow, not the thing itself.
The dead man has been asked about the thought of the barrow.
Not of a pushcart, not of the gardener, not of the farmer.
This red wheelbarrow sits pristine after rain.
The dead man can tell it is spring and all, it's the rain.
The dead man, stopping at the Williams home, read the
      medical shingle.
He did not take down the shingle and carry it to the classroom.
He did not bring the wheelbarrow to school.
Later, the dead man took *Spring & All* to Spain, the one book only.
He had time there to let the little wheelbarrow sit unused.
Thus did the dead man restore the dance of the red wheelbarrow.
Thus did he peel the layers of claptrap.
The dead man flexes his muscles, peels his eyes, licks his lips,
      sniffs briefly and opens his ears.
Then he takes the handles of the red wheelbarrow.

2. More About the Dead Man and "The Red Wheelbarrow"

The dead man hears them talking of "The Red Wheelbarrow."
He hears Williams repeat, "The word is not the thing."
To the dead man, the poem is itself, a dance, a complex of the
      sensory at a distance neither of time nor of space.
Albeit, it is as well a piece in a jigsaw of the imagination and a
      credo born of desire.
The dead man hath interred in the classroom the canon.
The dead man does not cease his dancing to name the tune.
The dead man places the red wheelbarrow next to a red wagon, in
      the garage with the silver roller skates, near a scooter made
      from a vegetable crate.
It is so clean, this unreal wheelbarrow, wetted, waiting,
      sacramental.
The dead man can hold in mind a red wheelbarrow and a blue
      guitar at the same time.
They are equally light in the ether.
Stevens was music, Williams was dance, the wheelbarrow was red.
The dead man rode the wheelbarrow and picked the guitar.
The dead man heard the music of the spheres even as he felt, also,
      the dance of the galaxies.
The dead man need not defend his turf, for he has drawn
      no boundary.
So much depended on the poem having no title.

THE BOOK OF THE DEAD MAN (RHINO)

Live as if you were already dead.

1. About the Dead Man and the Rhino

The dead man rode a rhino into Congress.

An odd-toed ungulate in the Congress, and no one blinked.

It was the lobbyist from Hell, the rhino that ate Tokyo, a lightning
    strike in their dark dreams.

A ton of megafauna, and nowhere for a senator to hide.

I'm gonna get you, says the momentum of a rhino.

The rhino has been said to stamp out fires, and the dead man
    hopes it is true.

He steered the beast to the hotheaded, the flaming racist, the fiery
    pork-barreler, the sweating vestiges of white power.

The dead man's revolutionary rhino trampled the many
    well-heeled lawmakers who stood in the way.

He flattens the cardboard tigers, he crushes the inflated
    blowhards, he squashes the cupcakes of warfare.

Oh, he makes them into blocks of bone like those of compacted
    BMWs.

2. More About the Dead Man and the Rhino

The dead man's rhino was not overkill, don't think it.

He was, and is, the rough beast whose hour had come round at last.

The dead man's rhino did not slouch, but impaled the hardest
      cases among the incumbents.

The committee chair who thought a rhino horn an aphrodisiac
      found out.

The dead man's rhino came sans his guards, the oxpeckers.

He was ridden willingly, bareback, he did not expect to survive, he
      would live to be a martyr.

The rhino's horn, known to overcome fevers and convulsions,
      cleared, for a time, the halls of Congress.

The senators who send other people's children into battle fled.

They reassembled in the cloakroom, they went on with their
      deal-making.

They agreed it takes a tough skin to be a rhino.

E BOOK OF THE DEAD MAN (THE RIVER)

Live as if you were already dead.

1. About the Dead Man and the River

The dead man stands on the bank of a river that overcame
     its banks.

He stands where the river has made a new road to ride.

He strides the shore and salutes the ones in boats looking to help,
     the homeowners returning in rubber boots, and the store
     owners who carried their inventory on their backs.

He pictures the convoy of artworks spirited away by night to the
     big city.

He doffs his cap to the sandbaggers and the boxers of books, and
     to those whose signatures can float a loan.

The dead man earlier hath seen the river complacent, he hath
     stopped it in time, he hath likened it to the curve of space.

He hath seen in it the impenetrability of time.

And if he must swallow hard nature's indifference, still the story
     was always about the planet, never about us.

Now he must witness the depth to which thinkers go not to say so.

Here is the mud so full of life forms, and now the river makes a
     deposit and backs away and makes another and turns and
     makes another and so on.

The dead man is bigger than the river only because he lives as if
     he is dead.

He is greater than the planet only because he lives as if he is
     pure energy.

What size shirt and cape fit a man of pure energy?

Does he wear galoshes or waders, does he stand on the water or
    slumber on the bottom, is he human?
The dead man stopped asking when he eased the separation
        between here and there, now and then, land and sea, angst
        and regret.
The dead man's life is about what is happening.

2. More About the Dead Man and the River

The dead man does not hold still for his portrait.

He stands at river's edge in a watery wind, as elsewhere he lay on
   thermal ground to dispute the horizon.

It was the thunder that crinkled the paper and his picture.

It was the water that erased it, the fire that made ashes of ashes,
   the air that carried them off, and the dirt that colored them.

The dead man has found a replacement for the self.

He has absorbed the solitudes that gather in crowds.

He has heeded the alarm of the crow and the bark of the rooster as
   they marked out the day.

Now he adopts a posture that pressures the edges of the picture, a
   bearing that disperses the one self, a carriage about to go.

How shall he throw out his arms if not akimbo?

How shall he be less than haphazard, less the dumb luck collector,
   less the random apocalypse that blinked from another galaxy?

The dead man is faceup to the sun and stars.

He is the longitude and latitude of his whereabouts, the wrinkly
   motto of his forehead, the tattoo in the mud attributed
   to aliens.

The dead man stands for a portrait that is all hello.

What would have been anything without the dead man?

It was history in the making when the dead man first appeared, he
   is the reason you turn the picture over to check.

Until the dead man, there was no water under the bridge, there was
   no past.

THE BOOK OF THE DEAD MAN (THE ROADS)

Live as if you were already dead.

1. About the Dead Man and the Roads

The dead man has taken both the high road and the low road.

He has traveled enough of the low road to have seen it awash in
the liquidity of the wealthy.

He has seen the waterlines on the houses of the poor who live low
for the rich farmland, the quick fish, the watery appraisals.

Now the dead man must live high, higher than the built-up
turnpike, higher than the bridges, above the condos and
roof gardens, above the belfries and steeples.

He must live above the rooftop water savers and exhaust fans
where the workers struck an American flag in better days.

He must live high to see who is coming.

Not the armies, not the rebels, not the educated rabid nor the
dismal who need to talk, nor the rampant criminal, nor any
creature with or without speech and self-thought.

That's right, the dead man has his head in the clouds.

The dead man knows that to be safe and awake one must be
everywhere and nowhere at once.

This the dead man can accomplish as only a living dead man can.

He looks down now, but not in judgment.

He is not of the critical masses, he is, rather, the first and the last,
the here and the gone, the always and the never, he is fit for
lifetimes beyond his own.

Let the man or woman who has perfect knowledge of the zero
and has seen the folly of the one find these writings in
the future.

For they are next, not previous, they are ahead not prior, they
    claim the territory beyond the sensate, they exceed the last
    frontier, they go.

2. More About the Dead Man and the Roads

The dead man is on time, though he disputes the notion.
The dead man is the purveyor of a clock face without hands, of a
      sundial for night, of starry pixels refreshing the sky.
It would be too easy for the dead man to buy into time.
It would be simple to say yes I know what you mean, if he meant it.
The dead man thinks the meaning is not what you mean.
It is not intention, nor success, not standing, not the hammer or the
      chisel, not the rock face or the river bottom.
It is not where you will go, but where you are.
Were you rash, and are you now rusty, were you sheepish, do you
      envy the vagabond?
Did you digress to wax nostalgic, and did you wise up?
It is not where you go but what you are.
The dead man likes the high road for its rattling pace, its
      single-mindedness, its web of isolate sensibilities.
The dead man likes the low road for its backtalk amidst acres of
      rubble, its überworldly sass, its animal ooze.
He has steered his way across hollows and knolls, on- and
      off-road, to the spiral exits and the blunt dead ends.
Now he has somewhere to go that isn't on the roads.

THE BOOK OF THE DEAD MAN (SCARS)

Live as if you were already dead.

1. About the Dead Man and Scars

There's a shiny scarring on the blade of the scissors where the
      dead man cut copper.

And a scar in the mirror, backward.

Where his elbow opened the door, there's an oval scar.

And a long scar on the cheek of his nemesis from the dream
      struggle.

There is a thin scar on the plate where the knife sawed too long.

And a scar in his throat just now from the hot soup.

The dead man could go on forever, listing his scars, but there's
      no time.

If there were time, which there never was, he could draw you a map.

He has scars inside and out, and a rattle in his head.

The dead man flexes his muscles and checks his scars in private.

2. More About the Dead Man and Scars

Outdoors in a dream, the dead man thought he was riding a bull,
    but it was only a gust of wind.
He thought he was hoofing it home, but it was his leg, twitching.
Never mind his nemesis, or his illusions, the dead man has an
    outlet, which is waking.
He wakes from the scarred world of dreams to a water-stained
    ceiling and streaked window glass.
His hand on the blanket is scarred from the time he gunned a
    motorbike downhill.
Oh, the dead man's scars are like bandages.
He is held together by the marked veins and arteries within him.
He waited out the scabs that became scars and scar tissue.
Now he is impenetrable.
Now he can open a door with his elbow and not feel a thing.

THE BOOK OF THE DEAD MAN (THE SHOVEL)

Live as if you were already dead.

1. About the Dead Man and the Shovel

The dead man steps on the shovel that will dig him up.

It's the dance a dead man does, with one foot on a shovel and one
foot in the grave.

The dead man is Nijinsky's understudy, he is the janitor at
La Scala, he is a stowaway on the freighter.

He is the underside of the surf, where a swimmer, pancaked by a
wave, is trying to breathe again.

With his shovel, the dead man digs a shoe and a scarf from
the snow.

Is it funny that the dead man fears being buried alive?

He shovels up an earth in which human parts are encased in
rectangles, cones and parallelograms.

His is the land rutted by oxen, gritty with crumbled pillars and the
torsos of clay gods.

He is a digger of graves, even his own, he is not shy.

You will know him by his spade, his scoop, his ladle, his love of
the Big and Little Dippers.

How natural to think him digging, dredging, excavating,
hollowing out, gouging, then burrowing.

The dead man is also the wood and pulp, the buried fish and
eggshells, all the totemic items sent to the afterlife.

He knows what the revered poet said about his son, and about you.

He knows what is useful and for how long.

2. More About the Dead Man and the Shovel

So now they want the dead man to tell them.

They want the juicy pieces, the drippings, the blood and the tears.

They think he can answer for the Absurd.

They think the dead man has caulked the places from which the
  hungers trickled, so that now nothing more matters.

They think it, because he abandoned distinctions, because he
  archived desire, but it is not so.

If only the dead man had found a dragon to slay, he might have
  returned us to moral zero, that's the myth.

None will know what the dead man whispered to the president
  with his cabinet still in the vestibule.

The dead man is equally the voice of the White House and
  the dollhouse.

Equally so, the dead man improvises a way to fit in.

Witness him shoveling soil by the magnolia, scooping ashes at the
  chimney, for he goes where the work is.

His loyalty to the present is the icing on the cake of our
  celebrations.

He is the one who will face off with those of forked tongues, the
  hurlers of brickbats, the professors of quagmire.

The dead man is mythic only because he is not too lofty to sink.

The dead man is not freaky, he is one of us, a shoveler.

Live as if you were already dead.

1. About the Dead Man and the Sun

The dead man has asked material things to speak of the sun.

The dead man is the one who fully embraces the sun.

He loves the throbbing ball of fire.

He feels the water rising to meet it, the earth absorbing it, the air spreading it.

Of the four elements, it is the sun of which he has the most experience and the fewest words.

The dead man has been visited in dreams by a fox, it was the sun.

He saw the wolf on the hilltop and the coyote in the valley, it was the sun.

Something like a large weasel crossed his path, it was the sun coating the black pelt with color.

The dead man hath unearthed the new words that can bring the sun closer.

He hath opened a bible to the Creation.

He hath walked by the bog and the lake to see the light drawn down and returned.

He hath looked into the mirrors of the water, the encapsulating canyon walls tanning at dawn, the green flash of sunset at the horizon.

The sun was in his eyes, so what did he see?

2. More About the Dead Man and the Sun

The dead man hears the sun hiss, what is that?

The sun has been personified as the head of an angel, can it be?

It has been thought of as desire, as wisdom, as an eye, as a
      passenger in Apollo's chariot.

All of it true in the lexicon of transcendent metaphor.

For the dead man, too, looks to make something more of the
      solar system.

He, like you, revolved around the parent, so it is like himself, is
      it not?

He, too, felt the heat and the light, he, like you, was sometimes
      blinded.

The dead man, of all men, suffers the poverty of language.

Let the sun sweeten the air beyond capture, let it be too little or
      too much, let it be white at noon and auroras at the poles.

We will know it by the halo of our heroes and heroines, we will see
      it in the sea and snow, we will devour it after harvest.

The dead man has written to the sun without words and without
      saying why.

The dead man's time has been more than half of the sundial.

He stays up late and later to look for the sun.

THE BOOK OF THE DEAD MAN (SUPERHERO)

Live as if you were already dead.

1. About the Dead Man and Plastic Man

Patrick "Eel" O'Brian, the dead man has been following you.

Like you, he has reached beyond his corporeal origin, that turf
     of sinkholes.

Like you, he was taught by the inmates of prisons and hospitals
     and those at sea in their heads.

Like you, he thought he could jump out of his body to be free, but
     he wised up.

He made his body more visible and familiar, more malleable,
     more osmotic, more heady and base, more painful, and yes,
     more plastic.

William James, writing past the threshold of consciousness,
     merely entered the realm of plasticity.

Plastic Man is the model, he of the pop-out eyes and rubbery
     shoulders, of the slingshot, of knots and bows, he the
     ensemble of the self.

Surely James knew automatic writing was only the perpetual
     morphing of a plastic consciousness.

Like this, like what you are reading, and seeing, and almost
     thinking.

A poem is about what is happening as you read it.

2. More About the Dead Man and Plastic Man

Patrick "Eel" O'Brian, you became the one who could reach for
      the moon.
The one who could hold his beloved's hand from afar.
You went straight.
We pictured the twisty road, the switchbacks of a life, the hard
      breathing in the passes, the sweating and the thirst.
We believed in you for thousands of years before you arrived.
The lever and pulley were stopgaps, the wheel and screw were
      expedient, we were on our way.
Later, the twisted stasis of the yogis, the whirl of the Sufis, the
      immobility of the monk were precursors to a new self.
The dead man is your true progeny.
He is the new self that is many.
He is the self defined by more than shape.

THE BOOK OF THE DEAD MAN (VERTIGO)

Live as if you were already dead.

1. About the Dead Man and Vertigo

The dead man skipped stones till his arm gave out.

He showed up early to the games and stayed late, he played with
abandon, he felt the unease in results.

His medicine is movement, the dead man alters cause and
consequence.

The dead man shatters giddy wisdoms as if he were punching
his pillow.

Now it comes round again, the time to rise and cook up a day.

Time to break out of one's dream shell, and here's weather.

Time to unmask the clock face.

He can feel a tremor of fresh sunlight, warm and warmer.

The first symptom was, having crossed a high bridge, he found he
could not go back.

The second, on the hotel's thirtieth floor he peeked from the
balcony and knew falling.

It was ultimate candor, it was the body's lingo, it was low tide in
his inner ear.

The third was when he looked to the constellations and
grew woozy.

2. More About the Dead Man and Vertigo

It wasn't bad, the new carefulness.

It was a fraction of his lifetime, after all, a shard of what he knew.

He scaled back, he dialed down, he walked more on the flats.

The dead man adjusts, he favors his good leg, he squints his best
       eye to see farther.

No longer does he look down from the heights, it's simple.

He knows it's not a cinder in his eye, it just feels like it.

He remembers himself at the edge of a clam boat, working
       the fork.

He loves to compress the past, the good times are still at hand.

Even now, he will play catch till his whole shoulder gives out.

His happiness has been a whirl, it continues, it is dizzying.

He has to keep his feet on the ground, is all.

He has to watch the sun and moon from underneath, is all.

THE BOOK OF THE DEAD MAN (THE VOTE)

Live as if you were already dead.

1. About the Dead Man and the Vote

The dead man was in the crowd when the militia moved in.

You can't know what the dead man who was there knows.

He was told to pipe down, to tread lightly, to wave when the
leaders passed on their way to the great hall.

He saw the past reemerge from the future, he saw midnight
at noon.

If a dead woman is walking on the street after an election and gets
shot, is that a vote?

And is beauty in the eye of the beholder, or shall we vote?

The candidate still wants to be in office when the Apocalypse comes.

The dead have voted, the injured have voted, those running from
the polling places have voted, and those awash in placards
have voted twice.

The dead man has voted with a pen, with a punch card, with a
lever, in ink and blood.

If there were more bread, we would not have to run through the
sewers clutching our ballots.

The dead man has seen the proud fingers of the illiterate, given
a vote.

He has stood on line with the gerrymandered, the disenfranchised,
the ones who walked miles to make a mark, the hopeful and
the fearful.

Shall the dead man choose among the old and new oppressors?

Shall he vote for the army, the navy, the palace guard, the elite,
  those with the common touch, the new paradigm or the
  public statuary?
The dead man and dead woman will be sending absentee ballots.
They are the root and branch, the stem and the leaf of a free society.

2. More About the Dead Man and the Vote

The dead man keeps his powder dry, his lamp turned low, and his
        eyes on the sky.
He hears the say-so of change in the breeze, he sees the
        calligraphic dance of the reeds, he smells the dust where
        people ran.
The dead man will speak, and all the dead will speak, for you
        cannot soap the mouths of dead men and dead women.
He can smell a cleansing storm coming while there are ashes on
        his tongue.
The dead man has strung together the unlikely.
The despot never sees it coming, even as the voters throw open the
        palace doors.
Now the dead man sits down to a meal of rice and kebabs.
He could be talking to his beloved, to an engineer, to the ghost of
        Alexander the Great, it is a muttering under his breath.
The dead man hath disputed every election.
He hath counted the petitions and depositions, he hath tallied
        the ballots.
He hath seen the final figures approaching zero.
He hath placed a pox on the parties equally, on the candidates
        equally, on the party-line masses.
For it is only the independent for whom the dead man will vote.
The dead man does not buy and sell his preferences.
He enlists the chaos, he joins the rabble, he leads the caucus,
        then leaves.
The dead man is free.

THE BOOK OF THE DEAD MAN (WARTIME)

Live as if you were already dead.

1. About the Dead Man in Wartime

The dead man, dead and alive at the same time, joins up.

Being both dead and alive, the dead man has nothing to lose.

The corpses that were kept out of sight of the president turn up in
the newspapers under their red, white and blue blankets.

The unregistered suicides at the front skew the casualty figures.

The number one adds up, the tens, the hundreds and thousands
and hundreds of thousands.

He cannot find enough wheelbarrows for the innards.

His spade is blunted from the digging.

The dead man is not loyal to America but to Americans.

The dead man was Lincoln's nightmare.

The dead man was a good combatant, he obeyed the orders that
took place in the dark.

He ran the straw dummy through with a polished bayonet.

His insignia shone.

When he tore off his gas mask, he said "Yes, sir" through his tears.

In the barracks, he was orderly, pristine.

For it was military to be headlong, then obeisant.

It was martial to be in step, then scattershot behind fields of fire.

His is the timeless courage of the eternal football player,
persuaded that the team can do more if it just wants to.

He is the lie embodied, the youthful will, the life force beheaded.

Okay then, when there is no weaponry sufficient, no final map,
no total casualty, no last report, no one uniform, no
happenstance that is not as deadly as the tracers, then there
is no end to it.
The dead man volunteers, he is needed.

2. More About the Dead Man in Wartime

One can take off the uniform, but it lasts forever.
You want the marching song, the rhythmic call-and-response.
No one leaves the army, dead or alive.
There are books.
The books tell you ahead of time how many will die in the
       first platoon.
They tell you the terrain, the weather, the time of attack, the
       forces necessary.
They tell you the aftermath of bullets, shrapnel, gasses and
       chain reactions.
Have you seen the artillery arching over the horizon — it is
       beautiful.
Have you witnessed the fireballs, heard the bass thuds of the
       mortars, and felt the recoil of the shoulder-held?
Did you wonder what it was like at the target?
Ask the dead man about the unstanched blood, the stench
       from amputation.
The dead man has carried the base plate of the inaccurate mortar.
He has slung the semiautomatic that is sure to hit something.
He has crouched in the spray of bullets, his finger still on
       the safety.
He has unpinned the grenade and cocked his arm like a pitcher
       with no target.
He has lobbed death into the distance without knowing where
       or why.

He has gone to the front and penetrated the lines, it was asked for.
He has rappelled the side of a cliff in a dark philosophical mood,
      it was training.
He has crawled on his belly without looking up.
He is of the infantry, he has a specialty, he is known by his
      dog tag.
Here are his boots, of a size to envelop two sets of socks.
He does what soldiers do to survive, you don't want to know.
Here, inside the rattling armored troop carrier, is a smuggled
      family photo.
The dead man touches the horror day and night, why don't you?
He will be going home.

THE BOOK OF THE DEAD MAN (WHITEOUT)

Live as if you were already dead.

1. About the Dead Man and the Whiteout

In a whiteout, in a gummy fog, the dead man dissociates.

An opaque breeze singes the foliage.

The dead man is himself a whiteout, an erasure, a palimpsest.

Here is not the artificial parchment of a drafting table, this is
      human skin loose on its binding.

You cannot see all of the dead man, nor can he know all of himself.

You see him in a fog under which you think there may be a sea.

You meet him in silhouette, you meet him cauterized by the sun,
      you reach to touch him and your hand goes on through.

The dead man's story is the page left blank, the bullet empty of
      powder, the ax insufficiently honed.

He looks bigger in outline, he gains stature when held in place.

He looks back, then hurries into the fog without a light.

2. More About the Dead Man and the Whiteout

He has been breathing in the air, that's what.
He remembers the look on your face, the lifted eyebrows, the
        anticipation that crossed your brow as he looked back.
Then he was eaten by the whiteout, leaving only an outline.
The dead man is not changing the future, that's what.
It is the last day of ten or the last year of millions, it is the last
        century or the final seconds, the past is disappearing,
        that's what.
Write it on the bark or the barn, spell it in the leaves, keep it in
        shadow, everywhere is a new page.
The dead man is as polarized by a whiteout as by a blackout.
Now he must wait for it to lift or find the other side.
Here is the dead man in a stupor, in a haze, a man of mist
        and murk.
He was out walking early when everything went blank.

THE BOOK OF THE DEAD MAN (THE WRITERS)

Live as if you were already dead.

1. About the Dead Man and the Writers

The dead man has been licking envelopes from the past.

The dead man's mouth is full of old glue.

He registers the poets starving for a yes, the option-dollars left
behind when a writer ran out of material, the trickle of
royalties during writer's block.

He lines up the empty wine bottles, the shot glasses, the
dead soldiers.

The dead man has made a pinch pot, a kiln god, a clay-footed
statue of a famous author.

He remembers the young writer who rediscovered the Mayans.

It was the Dadaists had it right, the Surrealists who knew what
was what, the Mayans, the Incans, the lost scribes of
Atlantis.

The young writer thinks someone must have known how.

The young writer is cast out of himself and lives between what he
was and what he may be.

The dead man and dead woman do the same.

Hence, the dead man ships his writings to the future.

He is still ten thousand fools, all the young writers at once.

He pitches the universe an idea of the sublime.

He opens his Shakespeare, what else? for a playmate.

2. More About the Dead Man and the Writers

The Sumerians had it, the Etruscans, they knew in antiquity what
    writing could be.
In lofts and basements, in woods or city, at the café or the tavern,
    the young writers live between old and new, between
    recovery and creation.
The dead man advises them to look past the words.
They open their Dante, what else? to feel what it is to be forlorn.
They roll and pitch on the deck of a rudderless self.
Are they self-similar, thousands more fractals of the natural world?
They gather with the like-minded to mimic, rebel and shape-shift.
They hunger for the wisdom of the dead, they fall for fools.
The dead man was one of you.
Like you, he was a part of the workshop in appearance only.
The dead man has gone to bed exhausted from finding words that
    could stay awake.
Then he recovered the Egyptians and Tibetans who wrote
    about him.
The dead man, like you, still writes into his ignorance.
That, and abandon, are the writerly attributes, but first he had
    a body.

THE BOOK OF THE DEAD MAN (YOUR HANDS)

Live as if you were already dead.

1. About the Dead Man and Your Hands

Mornings, he keeps out the world awhile, the dead man.

The dead man, without looking, believes what you said of
      the garden.

He knows the color of a rose is the color of a rose is the color.

He sees the early sky lit by a burn toward which we sidle.

He will take care of you, the dead man will do that.

He will wait for your hair to grow back.

He thinks the things you touched are lucky to be yours.

The dead man knows where to be and where not to be, how
      he survives.

He is aware, at all times, of your place, your dog, your rug, your
      roof, your chairs and tables.

Here is his own table, from the basement of the "as is" shop.

The dead man is of this old table, he is of his front and back doors,
      he is of the tea on the burner and the burner, too, he is.

It cannot stop the dead man, that others have caught on.

The dead man at his worst still looks his best.

2. More About the Dead Man and Your Hands

Nights, he lets in the world, the dead man does it, always.

By any late night, he has lost the need to believe.

The dead man plays a nighttime piano, he blows a nighttime horn,
      he sings more after midnight.

Dead man's music is nighttime, call it earthly, call it planetary.

The dead man feels the high registers heard by animal ears.

He feels the rumbly pedal note struck by redwoods enlarging and
      tectonic plates lurching.

What is it about his hands and your hands, is it the absence of
      certainty?

He has stirred distinctions into a broth, a soup, a stew, a gravy.

You cannot find yes and no, true or false, in a dead man's soup.

So what if they have caught on, the dead man is out front and stays
      up later.

Hence, when the dead man maketh eyes, he's gotcha.

He'll care for you, now that he's gotcha, and he hath giveth
      his hand.

He can't talk about the children if you are going to cry.

THE BOOK OF THE DEAD MAN (ZINE)

Live as if you were already dead.

1. About the Dead Man and the Zine

The dead man saw the one *Electronic Poetry Review* begin and end.

Given the start and the finish, the dead man can toggle the first
and the final.

For the Internet lasts forever, with Red Skelton and Martha Raye.

With Caruso, with Churchill, with Einstein inbound in sound
waves that consume the vacuum.

We in our space bubble can hear the past, we can recast it.

The revisions accumulate, invisibly, randomly layered in
dimensions beyond plane and direction.

We can go now, let's say, to the end point of each war.

We can see for ourselves the carnage morph into the bodies before
they were shredded.

The dead man has all of his faculties, and can smell and hear
those times of what is fondly called "yore."

The dead man, like others, must live in it and squeak.

When the dead man advises poets to stop whining, they hear it
wrong and think it means to stop drinking.

The dead man is able to hear through the static of wit
and nostalgia.

He tried but failed to cut a break in the Möbius strip of experience.

He fell on his face trying to lean over the edge.

It was denial made the rain sound like wind.

It was denial caused the poison to be sprayed on the crops.

The dead man has too many examples at hand.

It was a cinch in the time of the piezoelectric crystal-controlled
    oscillator.
Now the dead man looks in vain for the infinitesimal relay in the
    printed circuit of a microchip made of water.
The dead man knows what is coming.
With pieces of oneself planted, manufactured and cloned, people
    will live what is called "forever."
They will wonder what it was like to have been dead.

2. More About the Dead Man and the Zine

The dead man treasures the treasuries unburied and unlocked in
        the illusions of time.
For now the *Electronic Poetry Review* must shiver at the outskirts
        of sensibility.
It wobbles and flashes from the outpost of awareness.
It has turned sensibility inside out, there it is.
The dead man is of many minds, always was, and has lived to
        employ them all at once.
That is the dead man nature of the sentence in the indeterminate.
That is the *raison d'être* of the will.
Let the dead man record the demise of free will in the chaos of so
        many choices.
Now we know it all, all the time.
The dead man was happy to be fewer, for all that.
Now he is more than alive as the many.
It was denial that left string theory at loose ends.
It was denial that could not see the unified in disunity, the
        quantum disguised as inertia.
It was eyes, it was the holding action that kept us too close.
Now, as zines populate the cyberworld, the space remains endless.
The dead man pictures the Biggest Bang.
Imagine the imaginary type, the mathematics of a single
        black hole.
For it was always about the planet, never about us.
The dead man is at peace under the rocketry.

The pure pleasure of pixels lives on, nor all our piety nor wit can
cancel the binary yes and no of the method.
The dead man is the essence of on and off, of now and later, of
forever and not at all.
The dead man, at the end, turns a page.

ABOUT THE AUTHOR

Vertigo is Marvin Bell's twenty-third book. He and his wife, Dorothy, live in Iowa City, Iowa; Port Townsend, Washington; and Sag Harbor, New York.

 Since 1972, Copper Canyon Press has fostered the work of emerging, established, and world-renowned poets for an expanding audience. The Press thrives with the generous patronage of readers, writers, booksellers, librarians, teachers, students, and funders — everyone who shares the belief that poetry is vital to language and living.

Copper Canyon Press gratefully acknowledges board member

JIM WICKWIRE

for his many years of service to poetry and independent publishing.

MAJOR SUPPORT HAS BEEN PROVIDED BY:

The Paul G. Allen Family Foundation

Amazon.com

Anonymous

Diana and Jay Broze

Beroz Ferrell & The Point, LLC

Golden Lasso, LLC

Gull Industries, Inc.
on behalf of William and Ruth True

Lannan Foundation

Rhoady and Jeanne Marie Lee

National Endowment for the Arts

Cynthia Lovelace Sears and Frank Buxton

Washington State Arts Commission

Charles and Barbara Wright

To learn more about underwriting
Copper Canyon Press titles, please call
360-385-4925 X103

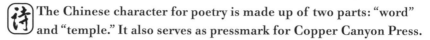The Chinese character for poetry is made up of two parts: "word" and "temple." It also serves as pressmark for Copper Canyon Press.

The text is set in Acanthus Text, designed by Akira Kobayashi in 1998 as a warmer version of Didot or Bodoni. Book title set in Alan Dague-Greene's Sirenne, also inspired by eighteenth-century typography. Book design and composition by Valerie Brewster, Scribe Typography. Printed on archival-quality paper at McNaughton & Gunn, Inc.